BETWEEN TWO WORLDS

BETWEEN TWO WORLDS

Aspects of Literary Form

A. E. Dyson

MACMILLAN
ST. MARTIN'S PRESS

© A. E. Dyson 1972

First published 1972 *by*
THE MACMILLAN PRESS LTD
London and Basingstoke
Associated companies in Toronto Dublin
Melbourne Johannesburg and Madras

Library of Congress catalog card no. 79–183545

SBN 331 13131 2

Printed in Great Britain by
WESTERN PRINTING SERVICES LTD
Bristol

For
GEORGE AND TINA COLE

Contents

Preface and Acknowledgements   ix

1   Between Two Worlds: Prologue   1

2   Virtue Unwavering: Milton's *Comus*   15

3   The Last Enchantments: Arnold's *The Scholar Gipsy*   41

4   Murderous Innocence: James's *The Turn of the Screw*   53

5   The Stranger God: Mann's *Death in Venice*   81

6   Faith among the Ashes: Scott Fitzgerald's
      The Great Gatsby   100

7   Trial by Enigma: Kafka's *The Trial*   114

8   Eagles and Trumpets: The Transmuted Experiences of
      Literature   135

9   Between Two Worlds: Epilogue   150

Index   153

Preface and Acknowledgements

This book is about literature, not about criticism, and I have tried to avoid 'the critical debate'. But a few general acknowledgements seem called for, and I am glad to name the critics who have influenced me most. First (among the moderns) Northrop Frye and C. S. Lewis; then, I think, the Geneva School, more indirectly than directly – Marcel Raymond, Georges Poulet, Jean Rousset, Jean-Pierre Richard, Jean Starobinski, and very particularly Albert Béguin, whose incarnational language links literary criticism most usefully outwards to the universal quest for religion, rather than inwards to the abortive romantic quest for the 'self'. Helen Gardner and Maynard Mack write beautifully, and often wisely; Frank Kermode's is a sparkling mind with which to disagree.

To name other living critics might be invidious, in times when so much good as well as bad criticism abounds. My more distant and chief debts are to T. S. Eliot, Coleridge and the whole tradition of literary Platonism and neo-Platonism, not forgetting – as I hope will be apparent – Plato himself.

The idea of this book has been in my mind for fifteen years, and parts of it have been published in earlier forms. I should like to thank the editors of *Essays and Studies 1955*, *Essays and Studies 1967*, *Modern Fiction Studies*, *Review of English Literature* and the *Twentieth Century*, and my co-editor of the *Critical Quarterly*, in whose pages material included here has appeared. All the chapters except the most recent one (on Mann's *Death in Venice*) have been extensively revised and rewritten, and the earlier versions are now superseded.

My thanks are also due to the many friends and students with whom I have discussed these topics over the years. The ideas and analyses are my own, but I have incurred more debts than I could record, or even remember.

April 1971   A. E. DYSON

I Between Two Worlds: Prologue

Form is everything. It is the secret of life. Find
expression for a joy, and you intensify its ecstasy. . . .
Have you a grief that corrodes your heart? Steep yourself in the language of grief, learn its utterance from
Prince Hamlet and Queen Constance, and you will find
that mere expression is a mode of consolation, and that
Form, which is the birth of passion, is also the death of
pain. . . .

. . . the artist, who accepts the facts of life, and yet
transforms them into shapes of beauty, and makes them
vehicles of pity or of awe, and shows their true ethical
import also, and builds out of them a world more real
than reality itself, and of loftier and more noble
import – who shall set limits to him?

Gilbert, in Wilde's *The Critic as Artist*

For you know that we poets cannot walk the way of
beauty without Eros as our companion and guide. We
may be heroic after our fashion, disciplined warriors
of our craft, yet are we all like women, for we exult in
passion, and love is still our desire – our craving and
our shame. Our magisterial style is all folly and pre-
tence, our honourable repute a farce, the crowd's belief
in us is merely laughable. And to teach youth, or the
populace, by means of art is a dangerous practice and
ought to be forbidden. . . .

Knowledge is all-knowing, understanding, forgiving;
it takes up no position, sets no store by form. It has
compassion with the abyss – it *is* the abyss. So we reject
it, firmly, and henceforward our concern shall be with
beauty only. And by beauty we mean simplicity, large-
ness, and renewed severity of discipline; we mean a
return to detachment and to form. But detachment,
Phaedrus, and preoccupation with form lead to intoxi-
cation and desire, they may lead the noblest among us to
frightful emotional excesses, which his own stern cult of
the beautiful would make him the first to condemn. So
they too, they too, lead to the bottomless pit. Yes, they
lead us thither, I say, us who are poets – who by our
natures are prone not to excellence but to excess.

From Aschenbach's Socratic reverie in
Death in Venice

I

Though these studies were written under separate promptings and at widely separated times, I have always thought of them as a group. But where was the link? The two poems and four tales proceed from different periods, temperaments and personalities. They range from the spiritual exhilaration of *Comus* to Kafka's deep gloom. The only inescapable similarity is their length. They are poems and tales poised between the 'short' and the 'long'.

But I had been attracted to them, it seemed, either for similar reasons, or in the same general region of response. Could anything useful be teased out of this? They are all works which have haunted my imagination for long periods, circling back at times with singular power. It is as though they are akin almost to those 'Proustian moments' which return through odd scents or sounds, chance associations, like mysterious keys to the inner self. They are all works which very much present 'themselves' to the imagination, so that what they say exists in union and tension with what they are. There is a world of expression, self-expression and communication, and a world of artefact, unprecedented and unique. The subject-matter links with 'life' and with much other literature, but the art resembles nothing but itself. In this they share common ground of course with all other works of art that achieve greatness, but with some quintessential qualities peculiar to themselves.

For these reasons, they press upon their readers certain lucid enigmas of literary form. What precisely is the relation of form to content in a work of literature? Does it chiefly resemble, or differ from, such a relationship in the other arts? Such questions require specific texts and suitable occasions; they require, perhaps, works like the six in question, on which a critic will willingly stake his claims for literature itself.

My procedure then is this. I offer six critiques, each standing (if it does stand) on its own feet, and range in the final chapters more generally afield. The six works point towards these larger issues: and, since a high claim is to be made for the value of literature and literary studies, I am glad to have them concretely to hand. They are not all 'religious' or all doubting; they are as varied in philosophy as their authors themselves. Certainly they are not rigged towards optimism, and would not serve as the basis for a creed. Their implicit and sometimes explicit views on the value of literature are diverse, and the prosecution case is compellingly put. But, equally, they share certain literary qualities across the gulfs which divide them; and these qualities – compression, a tension of opposites, symbolic resonance – characterise most works of literature that seem truly great.

II

While these works will be presented then in the next six chapters as autonomous, certain points of resemblance can be mentioned first. I want to examine in this prologue certain common aspects, which explain their joint appearance here.

My title 'Between Two Worlds' calls attention to two different polarities, which in certain aspects may be seen to link or even converge. There is a sharp contrast *inside* each work to be discussed between moral, psychological or experiential opposites; and there is that other sharp contrast, common to them all and to all works of art, between the world of 'content' and the world of 'form'. But in various ways the six central characters share something of the artist's creative dilemma, and become a partial paradigm of his formal concerns. The similarity is in the creative temperament itself, the creative ambition, which all of the six characters to some degree share. The difference however – an important one – is that, while none of the six characters achieves his creative and hoped-for fulfilment, the six authors in fact shape and present their work.

I want to think first of the internal and specific polarities, and to begin with moral aspects of the works. In two of them – Milton's and James' – we encounter a basic and traditional opposition between hellish evil and heavenly good. In Milton, the main moral bearings are supposedly unambiguous, though Milton knows that his tempters are clever and his readers confused. If Henry James's fable seems more intentionally complex, we can reflect that, though the author is not this time committed to an unambiguous 'hellish' and 'heavenly', as least he shares Milton's respect for devilish wiles. He knows how readily credulous mortals can be persuaded to mistake plain glass for mirrors or mirrors for reality, to look through binoculars, microscopes, distorting mirrors, and believe what they see.

In *The Scholar Gipsy* and *The Great Gatsby* the central polarities are also moral, but in the area where idyllic dreams collide with hard facts. Both works balance past against present, time against timelessness; their heroes hope to arrest or recapture perfection in defiance of change. Both works weigh an 'old' world against a 'new' historically – Arnold's with lyrical and delicate nostalgia, Fitzgerald's with richer glamour, sharper irony, harder despair. But, in both, the historical perspectives are incidental and not wholly integrated with the deeper fact of mortality itself. Arnold's 'strange disease of modern life' glances back to lost ages of faith and innocence, Fitzgerald's 'valley of ashes' invokes, for irony, the American dream. But the scholar gipsy and Gatsby are victims only marginally of the times they live in. More basically and inescapably, they are victims of Time.

When we turn to Mann and Kafka, it is to find that they undercut direct moral questions with polarities still closer to the purpose of life. Mann depicts an ageing artist caught up in the Bacchic experience; Kafka's hero moves in what might be nightmare reality, or nightmare dream. Are we to interpret Aschenbach as a man driven mad, or restored to sanity? Is Joseph K. locked in insanity, or awakened from sleep? Such questions confront totally alternative views of a soul in torment, and are antecedent to any moral bearings we may find. They remind us that these six works cannot be confined to simple moral distinctions, but probe the great dreams of truth by which men live. In this they invade one another's territory, and, when put together with one another or with other similar explorations, set up echoes among themselves. Milton weaves Bacchic spells in *Comus*, though not as Mann does; James's fable is as strange a report from the borderlines of sanity as *The Trial*.

III

The polarities explore moral vision and the ground of experience, but they are always dramatised in human terms. Each of these works involves at least one character whose main attempt is to re-arrange the 'reality' specific to the tale. Comus, the scholar gipsy, the Governess, Aschenbach, Gatsby and Joseph K. all move in their worlds as explorers, seeking to shape events. They hope to save or destroy themselves, or others, or, in the inner logic hidden from themselves, perhaps both. In this they have much in common with the artist who creates them, though only two are directly linked with the arts. They make common ground with their creators as prophets or lunatics, agents or victims, saviours or violators; as weavers of spells and dreamers of dreams. The very questions they prompt have an artistic fitness: are they good or evil, inspired or deluded? Given the chance, should we flee from them, or they from us? Or, we have to ask – since these works circle round the crux with special insistence – are they merely the supreme *exempla*, the pure instances, the quintessences demanded by art? The artist himself selects, shapes, refines and intensifies, and here, our six characters portentously share his quest. We are lured beyond a consideration of artistic intentions to the actual ambiguities of the creative mind. Was Milton really of the devil's party without knowing it? Did any of these writers fully control – even James – his finished work? We are referred back from 'intention' (knotty enough, as W. K. Wimsatt has shown us) to the still greater oddities of the creative mind. Is the artist himself prophet or fanatic, lunatic or truth-teller? Is *he* to be welcomed, or shunned? Is an artist 'really' Comus tempting the Lady, or the Governess saving her charges from the ghosts? Is he Gatsby wooing Daisy, or Aschenbach pursuing Tadzio? Is he the scholar gipsy abroad and elusive in Oxfordshire, or is he despite – or because of – his insight, Joseph K.?

IV

It will next be seen that if the author of each of these works stands in some degree of blood relationship with his central character, he does so in an especially ironic way. Though he creates and necessarily prescribes the 'reality' encircling his character, this 'reality' is profoundly unpropitious every time. 'Reality' is not attuned to Comus, the scholar gipsy, the Governess, Aschenbach, Gatsby or Joseph K., and their attempts to change – in K.'s case to understand – it are frustrated in decisive ways. This is the action on which we judge, or attempt to judge, the characters; and which we cannot evade when we judge, or attempt to judge, the work of art.

Before pursuing this, we can further note that Milton differs from the other five writers in that he offers not one but two leading characters, and that for one of them the 'reality' operative in the fiction *is* both propitious and true. Because the Lady is wholly good and moves among divine realities, her victory has an absolute quality which sets her apart. Alone of course among the six writers presented here, Milton is totally certain of his own moral bearings back in 'life'. As moralist, he celebrates the total triumph of good over evil; as artist, he celebrates the ways of God to man. Yet *as* artist, Milton creates with high imaginative intensity, and provides a world with its very distinctive laws. Readers are free therefore to explore any aspects which they strongly suspect to be unresolved or ambiguous; and, as Stanley Fish has demonstrated,[1] Milton possibly intended such an experience for his readers, to tutor their souls.

On this matter, views might differ; but the essential crux in our reading experience is the same. Though Milton's personal relationship to Comus is certain, and one of our data, readers are persistently split in their responses to the work. When we turn to Arnold in *The Scholar Gipsy*, it is to encounter a poet whose relationship with his central character is confessedly complex, and played off ironically against himself. The poet appears in his own poem as the scholar gipsy's well-wisher, nostalgic admirer, troubled half-believer; but, since troubled half-beliefs are worse than no beliefs at all to a high-minded agnostic, as his implacable enemy in the end. If the scholar gipsy is enjoined to 'fly our contact' for his safety, the 'our' most specifically includes the poet who brought him to life. When the poet makes his personal appearance in stanza 13, he is wholly alien to his hero's needs. The best Arnold can do, it seems, is to let the hero slip away under cover of a tremendous closing simile, to take his place – or so some critics have imagined – in the dubious reality of an 'eternal weekend'.

Some similarly troubled or even treacherous relationship might be sensed between Scott Fitzgerald and Gatsby, since Gatsby, although surrounded with glamour and almost certainly admired by his author, is never endorsed. Thomas Mann, of course, has an artist perceptibly close to himself as hero, but unresolved doubts are the essence of the tale. It may be that Mann writes very particularly to warn us against himself and against all other writers, and fails in this only by virtue of his own great success. What indeed could we pose against the deep doubts of Aschenbach's Socratic musings, if it were not for the indispensability of

[1] In *Surprised by Sin* (Macmillan, 1967).

Death in Venice itself? Henry James's Governess, it will be conceded, is an unparalleled creature; and the relationship of author to character, this time, I explore in the chapter to come.

A still more stark relationship between author and character is evidenced in *The Trial*, where not only the validity but the very possibility of successful structuring is cast in doubt. We cannot forget that the author who projected into the tale a *persona* not unlike himself as hero-victim wanted his book itself to be posthumously destroyed. The assertion of meaninglessness and disorder inside the tale would have been most strikingly endorsed had this last instruction to his friend Max Brod been obeyed. Yet, short of the work actually being destroyed, it exists as reality; so *The Trial* becomes an especially pertinent text for the triumph of art. Gambling, no doubt, on Max Brod's expressed unwillingness to obey him, Kafka lacked the final resolution to destroy his own art. While K. himself then is first victim, and later nobody, his creator could not undo creation and share K.'s fate. Left in existence, *The Trial* remains a superbly organic testimony to those very principles of reason, concern, structuring that it tries to deny.

There is in this a splendid irony, since hopelessness cannot, after all, be affirmed in a work of art. The more powerfully indeed the work uses all its art to create the illusion of meaninglessness, the more conscious of meaning in art we shall necessarily be. If these qualities were really absent or non-existent, how could they pass from the artist, through a verbal artefact, and live in our imagination as they do? To experience art is necessarily to experience as a human being, responding to triumphant creativity, resilience, communication from a fellow mind.

For a critic who holds the views which I shall put forward in my two final chapters, this is a reassuring fact. All art incarnates, among other things, the creative process, which is itself symbolised in what it makes. The artefact is indeed modified and transformed, by its symbolic status, in a direction inalienably connected with life and hope. But just as no literature can deny the intelligence, creativity and resilience which inform it, so no reader can deny these qualities without telling a lie. Our response to art must be creatively human, and so – this point I shall return to – in itself evidence of one, most important, aspect of the nature of man.

During the 1960s, many writers were obsessed by the desire to make art in fact deny itself, by asserting the absolute reality of what Mann called 'the abyss'. And artists bent on this effort can go a long way towards succeeding, as the works of Genet, Burroughs and many other moderns show. They can write tawdry erotica disguised as 'social realism' or 'psychological' insight, debasing language and therefore humanity along with themselves. They can depict the freedoms of civilisation and call these bondage, or the bondage of human vice and call this free. They can represent men as helpless victims of an absurd universe, and assert that communication itself must always fail. They can produce a violent and murderous vision of man and call it 'life-enhancing'; they can proclaim that meaning is nonsense and that nonsense is art. All such achievements point in the desired direction, but they cannot, by their nature, quite reach the goal. Since the only real denials are silence and suicide, art cannot fully become compatible with these. Any art which successfully makes its point is successfully structured, and cannot evade the irreducible evidence of itself. Even destroyed art – if art is destroyed – is no exception: if Max Brod had in fact destroyed *The Trial* so that we now had no knowledge of it, he would merely have concealed an artistic triumph and so told a lie.

What art *is* may, then, be a world in extreme tension with its content, though the worlds of 'content' and 'form' are always mutually transformed. The new entity certainly belongs to a realm we call 'fiction': but to see fiction as a move away from reality, a mere consolation (surely a false one?) for unstructured suffering, is to overlook its prime and greatest reality as art.

v

Such reflections turn on the ways in which 'form' not only can, but must, modify 'content'; and Chapter 8 will concern itself with some of these. For the moment my purpose is to offer a simple reminder of the many individual ways in which what a work 'says' might be implicitly denied, or actually completed, or wholly transcended by what it 'is'. Form infuses the tale with appropriate beauty, conferring a sense of completeness or inevitability upon the whole. And we sense this not only in the formal ending, or when the work is recalled in retrospect or in later readings, but during the process of reading itself. There are clues of tone, genre, structure, ironies, overtones, resonances, from the moment we read the first lines. We know what kinds of irony will operate in *Death in Venice* before Venice is mentioned, just as we know how wholly these will differ from the ironic potentials of Comus's wood, Gatsby's New York, or Bly. In some sense, the critical mind grasps 'the whole' with foresight while reading closely, and the unfolding work might evolve its own ironic tension with what is rightly foreseen. The literary tone or flavour created through every verbal and linguistic aspect contributes to our vivid and particular sense of the whole.

What I am touching on and shall return to after the analyses, is the manner in which the world of human experience – which art mirrors, and recreates, and cannot if it is great art falsify – turns into particular and autonomous art. There is our general sense that any striking book belongs not only to the landscapes of life which it mirrors, but to that quasi-eternity of achieved and unchanging form. As we look at the bound volume of Keats on the shelf or the title *Edwin Drood* in a catalogue, some timeless incipience is invoked. There they wait, the words on the page, in immutable order; and locked within them, the life and intensity, the vision and power. All the people and places are there, like the dead heroes of Yeats' 'Easter 1916': 'Enchanted to a stone/To trouble the living stream'. But, as T. S. Eliot pointed out, the order of literature is not entirely unchanging: great works modify one another, co-operating with those changes which the progress of history itself infuses into the past. And individual readers differ, each contributing a range of experience, a range of temperamental quirks, personal verbal associations, which make his responses inevitably unique. Yet, beyond all this, art certainly partakes of the changeless, in the prime reality of its created life. The artefact stands outside time, potent with vitality, arrested yet available, for as long a time as its physical existence continues and there are minds to respond.

We recognise this world of art, this world of literature; and alongside it, a series of worlds peculiar to the artists themselves. When writing of Graham Greene, Laurence Lerner spoke of 'Greeneland': by which he did not deny of course that Greene writes of real places and real people, but pointed rather to the distinguishing flavour of Greene's art. The worlds of Milton James, Mann, Kafka – of all great writers – are highly distinctive, and like nothing else we can recall. In addition, there is a further world of individual masterpieces with many nuances peculiar to themselves. The wood where the Lady meets Comus; the scholar gipsy's Oxfordshire; Bly; Aschenbach's Venice; Gatsby's mansion; the working-class flats where Joseph K. goes to seek his accusers: we know these almost as we know our own homes. We know their special feel, their extraterrestrial geography, their habitat permanently suspended outside and above normal time. These aspects are the 'world' specific to literature, even while they relate back, firmly and clearly, to the 'real'. The artist cannot falsify reality if he is a great artist: yet his truest insights are, in their artistry, unique. The 'real world' is necessarily transmuted, and exists 'between two worlds' in this sense.

The title of this book will then find its centre in this area, where the general and the particular most hauntingly unite. While writing of any particular poem or book, a critic might take the union for granted; yet it is by no means certain that all critics do. My impression is that some critics not only ignore but even overlook it; and this includes all who, treating books as fictionalised history, sociology or psychology, overlook their prior status as art. Such criticism necessarily distorts and undervalues literature, even when the critic's intention is to praise. One characteristic fault can be the overlooking of beauty, which might be disregarded, or even denied. It is a supreme irony that a critic might even use the content of literature to assert life's dreariness or ugliness, while ignoring the final tribute to beauty and colour in art itself. Perhaps a surgeon concerned only with minute and delicate operations might ignore his patient's beauty; but what can we say of critics who make this mistake?

VI

I can best illustrate my own feelings about the union of worlds in literature through a reference to the symbolist phrase, 'All art aspires to the condition of music'. While listening to music, we know beyond argument that the emotional content cannot be paraphrased or transposed. It can, of course, be talked about – but this is discourse of a different kind. We apprehend moments of nostalgia, heroism, exuberance, exquisite tenderness, and can record or discuss these in general terms. But however much Wagner's *Ring* or Mahler's symphonies flood us with such feelings, we value these works chiefly for themselves. If they disappeared from the world, nothing could replace them; something would be missing beyond recall. The component feelings would still exist, and so would other splendid embodiments, but a most valued experience would be no more. The clarinet entry in the slow movement of Brahms's Second Piano Concerto is irreplaceable. There are other manifestations of piercing beauty, revelatory tenderness, but there is nothing else like that. Music is full of tragic heroism, apocalyptic revelation, but there is only one Immolation of Brünnhilde, only one proclamation of 'Hostias' in Verdi's Requiem, only one Beethoven Ninth.

On such matters there can be no argument, and certainly none that jumps back from art to 'life'. We value music, great paintings, King's College Chapel not only for the beauty and life inherent in them but, more particularly, for what they are. They may convey sharply to us other fine experiences, but the experience we value most is themselves. In this, they are as irreplaceable as people, and as unique in their power to move us to love.

It is a disadvantage, peculiar among the arts to literature, that this supreme and prime truth so often gets lost. We can fall into the error of assuming that a poem or novel is important only as one among many expressions of, or pieces of evidence from, 'life', and not at all or only very marginally for itself. Literature can be mistaken for raw material of history or sociology, so that those who love it – the real students of literature – might even find themselves abused for their pains. To assert that *Death in Venice* is a unique and precious masterpiece is to risk being accused of 'aestheticism' in some disabling sense. But this is not a mistake that could be made about anyone who claimed in this manner to value Bach's Mass or the 'Mona Lisa', which are instantly seen to be perfect and durable in themselves. We may value them in part for the new things they show us about the Christian Mass or about a certain kind of face smiling, but clearly we do not value them simply for this.

For this reason, my approach to art is essentially formalist, and it is the forms themselves that I value most. Because works of art are incarnate and yet also transform their creator's consciousness, they are among life's ends as well as its means. In this sense they are symbols of humanity, and symbols which may influence our

philosophy, indeed our religion itself. In recent years, there have
been many good critics of the novel (David Lodge, Graham
Hough, Frank Kermode and others) who have rightly stressed its
mimetic function, but the present balance errs none the less to
that side. My own stress will accordingly fall on the artefacts, and
on the life and hope inherent in these.

VII

A contrast of worlds is, then, both the internal theme of the six
works now to concern us, and the continual challenge presented
in transmuting form. And this returns us to those allied questions
concerning the validity and value of art which all these six very
explicitly present. How can the fluid, muddled world of human
transience be indissolubly united to the static, pure, eternal or
quasi-eternal world of artefact and form? Are those who make
such unions prophets and saviours, or are they liars and frauds?
Clearly, the marriage changes both partners; but is the new union
edifying? Can it save? Does it achieve truth beyond the ordinary
– is it (as I am asserting) itself a truth beyond the ordinary – or
does it necessarily cheat and lie? The union as we have said
changes both partners, but is it a marriage or just a scandalous
affair? For Milton there can be no doubt that the artist is prophet,
but we hear a different tale from Mann.

There is a sense, of course, in which imagination in any artist is
bound to be an alternative to personal life. As Yeats says, there
is a perfection of the life and of the art; but if the art is to be perfect, there must be some degree of sacrifice of the life. And this
is not just a matter of time and energy directed and dedicated,
but of the artist's priestly isolation from his fellow men. It concerns the kind of attention, of contemplation, analysis and recreation, which he necessarily interposes between the experience
which 'goes into' the art and the art which results. The imagination becomes in an inescapable way its own hero, while its very
power to work, shape, move experience through refined insights
towards an intuited ideal, arrests the actual processes of life. The
early romantic poets had great confidence in the imagination, and
most of them saw it as an operation of the divine. And indeed I
share this confidence, as I shall indicate later; though with the
reservation that only a Platonic or Christian universe can give to

the imagination a fitting home. Later in the nineteenth century, there were doubts about the imagination's divinity, followed by inevitable redefinitions of its 'truth'. Henry James insisted that 'real life' should be banished just as soon as it had provided a clue to a story, to be replaced by the refining and intensifying processes of art. As soon as some chance word, anecdote, impression provided the 'germ' for his story, imagination had to take over from random flux. The truth of art became its concentration, its quintessences: but, since quintessences are after all not lifelike, art must to this necessary degree be removed from the normally 'true'.

By the same token, the artist's own 'real experiences' must suffer ironic displacements. Because he cannot live up to the ideal forms of experience imposed in the imagination, he becomes more than usually aware of mortality and flux. An Oscar Wilde, a James or Forster, might gallantly attempt to make life an art, to live art, but there must always be other voices to sing a cynical tune.

Such perplexities are to some extent reflected in all the central characters we shall now be meeting, who share not only their creator's propensity to shape, explore and intensify, but the ironic displacements of his life. Comus, the scholar gipsy, the Governess, Aschenbach, Gatsby and Joseph K. all in differing modes and with different kinds of failure aspire towards fulness of consciousness, freedom, self-fulfilment, in defiance of the unalterable limits set by the world in which they move. They all aspire to some degree of divinity (in K.'s case, to some degree of normal humanity), and explore bitter ironies of defeat. All of this might be a paradigm of the artist, who soars to the heights only to tumble down. Wilde might celebrate art as superior to life and therefore justified, but Mann will insist that art is after all a lie. *Tonio Kröger* (1903) is possibly the most savage indictment of art by a young artist ever made. Though the hero pursues high perfection and is drunk with beauty, his own life is squalor and mess. The readers he attracts are failures, who use his art as a revenge against life; the readers he covets, the 'blue-eyed ones', ignore him – and rightly, since he could only do them harm. Since the artist wears the mark of Cain and is akin to the charlatan, it is right that fathers should guard their children against him and bar their doors.

These indictments are all in part echoed in the works to concern us here, which therefore become doubly challenging to a critic intent on high claims for art. Arnold's poem concerns a mythical figure dedicated to simplicity who turns out to be impossible; James's tale a very strange and messianic heroine, Mann's a noble artist ruined by the god he must serve. Fitzgerald gives an artist's dream of grandeur to a tawdry gangster, Kafka gives an artist's exploration of reality to a man hounded to death. And even in *Comus* such ironies are not evaded, since the richest poetry is used for juggling and given to monsters. It might seem as if a really optimistic view of art would have to exist in defiance of these works rather than in vindication of them; yet my own sense of the great claim to be made for literature belongs to nourishment by these and their like over many years.

2 Virtue Unwavering: Milton's *Comus*

> Virtue that wavers is not virtue, but vice revolted from itself, and after a while returning.
>
> Milton: From *The Reason of Church Government Urged Against Prelaty* (1642).

I

Comus is itself enchanting, and a fine introduction to Milton. Many of the poet's rhetorical and stylistic techniques, and certain moral ideas which are central to *Paradise Lost*, *Paradise Regained* and *Samson Agonistes*, can be found in this early and glorious masque. By now it has had much critical attention, but certain accounts of a quarter of a century ago still prescribe the terms of debate. A full and valuable analysis was offered by A. S. P. Woodhouse in his article 'Argument of Milton's *Comus*',[1] but this erred, I think, on the side of being too elaborate and speculative. Mr Woodhouse discovered several levels of meaning in the poem, but he made far too much of the closing section, and his approach was more intensively intellectual than the text seems to me to warrant. In one positive respect, too, his emphasis was misleading. He maintained that the action of the poem is set in the realm of 'Nature' until the closing pages, when the entry of 'Sabrina fair' raises it to the realm of Grace. But to my mind, the visions of life belonging to Nature and Grace respectively are present side by side throughout the poem, the one represented by the arguments of Comus, and the other by the type of insight and strength which protect the Lady. The fact that in dramatic terms Comus's view, though plausible, is shown to be false, and the Lady's view, though austere, to be true, is central to the poem's meaning, and what it is really about. The word 'Nature' is handed over to the Bacchic experience and philosophy, and contrasted with the reborn 'nature' of Grace.

A more useful attempt would, I think, be to analyse the poem more simply in terms of the probable impression which an educated seventeenth-century audience would have formed on seeing a

[1] 'Argument of Milton's *Comus*'. *Toronto Quarterly*, XI (1941); '*Comus* Once More' *Toronto Quarterly*, XIX (1950).

dramatic presentation for the first or second time (though not necessarily at first performance, where the nature of the occasion, and the actors, would have intervened). This sort of analysis might avoid the pitfall of over-subtlety, and serve as a better guide to the main Platonic tenor of Milton's mind.

Dr Tillyard was one of the first critics to study *Comus* in detail,[1] and it is from his findings that I propose to differ here. Despite some points of interest in his interpretation, he seems to have misunderstood the main movement of the masque. Like Mr Woodhouse, he ascribes to the Epilogue, especially in its revised form in the 1637 edition, an importance altogether exaggerated. He finds in it a significance which only a scholar who knows the text, quite literally, backwards, is likely to consider convincing. When *Comus* is transferred from the study to the stage, the main outline of its ideas, action and moral purpose unfolds gradually from the opening words; and the total effect of the masque is not only firmly established by the time that Sabrina makes her appearance, but practically finished and rounded off as well. The closing moments have indeed their importance, but more for the exquisite lyrical relief they provide after the action than for any new ideas which they introduce or for any vital modification of the total effect.

II

The interpretation of *Comus* centres upon what we make of the case between Comus and the Lady. Dr. Tillyard assures us that previous attempts to consider this case had been wrecked by the assumption that 'one of the disputants is right'. The assumption, he argues, is false. 'Comus and the Lady are both wrong, or, if right, in ways they did not perceive.' He bases this assertion on the belief that to accept the Lady at face value is to accept Chastity as a mode of life more excellent than Marriage; and he argues from passages inserted in the 1637 version of the Epilogue, as well as from personal conviction, that Milton did not himself believe this to be true. I shall offer later my own tentative feelings on the early Milton's view of chastity; but I wish to say at once (and J. C. Maxwell agrees with this) that in my reading of the poem the Lady stands not so much for Chastity as for self-control,

[1] 'The Action of *Comus*', in *Studies in Milton* (Chatto & Windus, 1951); originally published in an earlier version in *Essays and Studies 1942*.

nsight, moral balance – or, to put this slightly differently, that
she does not stand for a particular virtue but for Virtue itself.
Milton does, in fact, choose Chastity for his particular virtue,
and I think this choice was more than arbitrary. There
s evidence that, as an idealist in the Platonic tradition, he
regarded it as the most important virtue of all. If the material
world is transient and tinged with illusion, then the virtue
which most clearly asserts that love arises in the soul and is ful-
illed there will be the virtue most immediately linked with
spiritual ascent. As Milton put it in *An Apology for Smectymnuus*
1642:

> Thus, from the laureate fraternity of poets, riper years and the
> ceaseless round of study and reading led me to the shady
> spaces of philosophy, but chiefly to the divine volumes of Plato
> and his equal, Xenophon: where, if I should tell ye what I
> learnt of chastity and love, I mean that which is truly so, whose
> charming cup is only virtue, which she bears in her hand to
> those who are worthy (the rest are cheated with a thick intoxi-
> cating potion which a certain sorceress, the abuser of love's
> name, carries about), and how the first and chiefest office of
> love begins and ends in the soul, producing those happy twins
> of her divine generation, knowledge and virtue – with such
> abstracted sublimities as these, it might be worth your listening,
> readers. . . .

In *Comus* then, Chastity is more than an isolated virtue: it is
symptomatic of spiritual wholeness and the life of grace. And at
the same time it is a special case, albeit the most important one, of
that classical as well as Christian issue touching human dignity
and salvation, the control of the passions by Reason. The great
debate in *Comus* (and 'debate' is a misleading word: the issue is
represented dramatically, and the actual debating points made by
Comus and the Lady are to be seen and judged in the context of
the poem as a whole) – the great 'debate' is not between Chastity
and Incontinence, and still less between Virginity and Marriage,
but between Reason and Passion as controlling factors in human
conduct. These factors are of course doors to reality, and through
them we pass to our personal experience of heaven and hell.

The centrality of this theme in seventeenth-century literature
have been impressed upon us by Dr Tillyard himself, and the intellectual ingredients of Milton's thought are well enough known.

The predominating influence was always Platonism, of the kind everywhere suffusing his early prose and verse. In the fragment 'On Time', he contrasts the dull and gross world of changing things with the purity and joy of eternity. The power of Time extends only to bad and worthless things. All that is good and true is meant for the realm of timeless perfection. When Time has purged away all that it has power to purge,

> Which is no more than what is false and vain,
> And merely mortal dross (ll. 5–6)[1]

then that which remains will be

> ... everything that is sincerely good
> And perfectly divine ... (ll. 14–15)

As for Man's end, the poet tells us that

> ... all this earthy grossness quit,
> Attired with stars, we shall for ever sit,
> Triumphing over Death, and Chance, and thee, O Time
> (ll. 20–2)

The word 'grossness' typifies Milton's identification with 'Earth' and the earthy life of all human passions that link man with the animal and lower parts of creation.

Another powerful theme in the early poems is the Platonic vision of cosmos as harmony and chaos as disharmony. 'Arcades' combines the two familiar commonplaces that the heavens are filled with music, but that only the virtuous can hear it:

> Such sweet compulsion doth in music lie,
> To lull the daughters of Necessity,
> And keep unsteady Nature to her law,
> And the low world in measured motion draw
> After the heavenly tune, which none can hear
> Of human mold with gross unpurgèd ear ... (ll. 68–73)

In 'At A Solemn Music', the specifically Christian version of this notion accounts for our earthly exile from the cosmic harmony as one of the consequences of Original Sin. The poet celebrates the celestial music, and prays

> That we on earth with undiscording voice
> May rightly answer that melodious noise;

[1] All quotations are from Douglas Bush's *Milton: Poetical Works* (Oxford Standard Authors).

As once we did, till disproportioned sin
Jarred against Nature's chime, and with harsh din
Broke the fair music that all creatures made
To their great Lord . . . (ll. 17–22)

Such themes pervade *Comus*, where the movement of the entire
drama is intended to illustrate them through our unwavering perception that the Lady's vision is true and Comus's false. As a
seventeenth-century Christian, Milton did not of course hold the
view that all ideas are equally fallible, or that 'Truth' is to be
found in or through a synthesis of opposites. Though he was far
from naïve – perhaps indeed because of this – he believed that
such distinctions as good and bad, white and black, true and
false can be made, and that they are of the most vital importance
to man. As a Puritan he held a profoundly theological view of
human nature and human history – a view which was the basis
of the political ideals and revolutionary hopes expressed in his
early prose tracts, and was firm and clear enough to inspire the
white heat of apocalyptic expectation to which these ideals
and hopes gave rise. He believed that, though certain common
arguments and actions are notoriously a mixture of truth and
falsehood, there is no necessary reason why this should be so. The
confusion is a consequence of the Fall of Man, not a reflection of
ambiguity and contradiction in the nature of things. In the last
resort, and to the recipients of a divine revelation, truth is both
knowable and known. A great gulf is eternally fixed between
God and Satan, Heaven and Hell, Pride and Humility – between,
in fact, Good and Evil, in their final and absolute forms.

Milton further believed that the Devil and his emissaries are
deceivers, and that the evil which they advocate is seldom
without strong arguments and inducements in its favour. Their
arguments, moreover, are not only subtle and well thought out,
but also not without the support of plausible though misguided
analogies drawn from the natural order. Satan in *Paradise Lost*
is at pains to suggest to Eve that God really wants her to eat the
apple, and that a correct understanding of her position as a free
being should make this clear. Comus, in the masque, argues with
great power that the whole cosmos sings his view of life, and that
it is the Lady, by her abstemiousness, who is out of tune. Both the
deceivers do much more than tempt the emotions. They tempt the
mind itself to confuse truth and lies.

Milton further believed that the arguments of devils were particularly likely to appeal to fallen man, whose understanding is clouded by the effects of sin so that he cannot clearly distinguish good from evil, and his will infected so that he is more than half in love with sin. As Stanley Fish has brilliantly argued, all Milton's major poems are partly intended to educate the reader into a clearer understanding of his own fallible and gullible responses as fallen man. The notion of 'truth' as a discovery made by the intellect alone would have struck Milton as nonsensical. Spiritual truth is seen by the eyes of the spirit, and reserved, as the Cambridge Platonists also insisted, for the pure in heart. Those who rely on their intellects alone will fall ready victims to the rationalisations and sophistries of devils. But the pure, who see the landscapes of heaven around them, cannot be made to doubt the truth of their hearts.

Milton did not, therefore, make the mistake of underestimating the diabolical mind, any more than he failed to see the limits of its power. In his representation, which is also the traditional one, evil is not unsubtle but unrealistic; not unintelligent, but wrong. To anyone equating 'truth' with the intellect and intellectual prowess with the result of an I.Q. test, this may seem puzzling; but our modern empirical view (perhaps no longer modern, and already fading) is at variance with the Christian and Platonic insight that, since purity and moral discipline are the doorways to knowledge of good and evil, this is a knowledge which no exercise of the discursive faculties, however capable, can hope to attain.

When Milton gave a devil or tempter his intellectual due, then, he was far from admitting that there might be 'something in' what was being said; and when he gave them their emotional due, in that their temptations really are tempting and not mere *tours de force* of abstract logic, he was not revealing an inward sympathy with sin.

But to some people, it appears, Milton is hardly worthy to be thought a serious artist if he was entirely free to reject the evils he drew. The very idea of the artist seems to them to imply pagan or diabolical affinities, or at the least some sympathy with what Thomas Mann calls 'the abyss'. This matter will recur, of course, in later chapters; but we can note here that the artist who prepared himself over years to write the greatest divine epic in

human history would not see his role, vis-à-vis devils and tempters, in so ambiguous a light. Though there were not to be any bohemian affinities in *Comus* – not if Milton could help it – there
were certainly to be the allurements and attractions proper to exemplary vice. No one can accuse Milton of making Comus less
than attractive, or of creating a devil too obviously unacceptable
in human eyes to be up to his task. Like Satan indeed, Comus has
striking arguments to use in his tempting, and splendid verse to
help him set them out.

My assumption therefore, bearing all this in mind, is that in a
moral or theological debate between good and evil Milton would
be certain to believe one side of the case, despite his ability very
forcibly to present the other, and despite his sense that richly
sensuous verse is more appropriate in a moral work to the bad
dramatis personae than to be good. Dr Tillyard rightly pointed
to the use of rhetoric in *Comus* and to the poem's affinity with
an academic disputation, but wrongly concluded that Milton is
in an impartial and midway position between the arguments used.
On some issues, no doubt Milton did suspend judgement, and
find the technique of arguing more interesting than the arguments themselves. But in matters of the sort which are at issue in
Comus he would inevitably have been deeply involved. The arguments which he gives to Comus (and to Satan) are not exercises in
rhetoric but insights into evil. To suppose for a moment that they
can be anything other than this is to get the whole poetry out of
perspective.

An example of Milton's rhetorical powers used more or less for
their own sake is to be found in 'L'Allegro' and 'Il Penseroso',
which, as Dr Tillyard has shown, *can* be regarded as academic
exercises, the one in praise of day and the other of night. But even
here Milton writes of familiar moods, more delightful and imaginative that the phrase 'academic exercise' perhaps suggests.
'L'Allegro' celebrates pagan and sensuous life – it could be a song
of Comus; 'Il Penseroso' longs for a secluded and scholarly life,
far from the crowd. Milton well knew that these were moods, not
programmes, and that to idealise them as ways of life was an em-
broidery of truth. Since the poems are day-dreams, there is no attempt to link them, or to engage them in a dialectic tug-of-war.
Milton does his best for each mood in turn, devoting his intelligence, fancy, art to 'making a case'. But in *Comus*, such cases

are set in a moral and dramatic context, where far more than pleasing fancies are at stake.

There are a few other general considerations relevant to *Comus*, which should be mentioned, however briefly, at the start. C. S. Lewis in his *Preface to 'Paradise Lost'*, observed that all artists find it easier to depict the bad characters than the good. For the former, a writer has only to look within himself, and to dramatise many of the instincts and desires he would normally suppress. For the latter, he has to depict a moral balance and perfection which in his own life most likely eludes him, and which may be less attractive, less imaginable indeed, to fallen man than the gravest of sins. If we think of the Lady in *Comus* as less attractive than Comus – if we find her prudish, or violent, or too coldly militant (such faults have been mentioned) – then C. S. Lewis's caution should be kept in mind.

The related problem is that a poet finds passion easier to portray than reason, if only because his rich verse is passionate in itself. Reason too can have its intensities, but like Dryden later, Milton could not always translate these into verse. In my opinion the bareness and austerity of Milton's verse when he was writing speeches for the Lady (and later for God the Father in *Paradise Lost* and for Christ in *Paradise Regained*) is not necessarily inferior, when read dramatically, to the sort of verse which he creates for Comus and Satan. But the verse spoken by Comus is undoubtedly more immediately attractive than that of his intended victim; and the emotional nature of his appeals conditions this.

We should remember also that it is easier for Milton to create an advocate of falsehood than an advocate of truth, easier to create Comus's frivolity than the Lady's 'high seriousness'. Comus and his crew are liars, like Satan after them, and can say practically anything that comes into their heads. As long as they have a practical aim in view, they can rationalise and defend it as freely as they wish. Saving only that their arguments must be intelligent, plausible, and at least superficially attractive, they can range wherever they will. This allows very great scope for passionate declamation, rich sensuousness, persuasive logic and all the poet's other arts. But God in contrast, and the angels and good characters, are limited to severely true statements and modes of thought. They have to be not only plausible and attractive but right – and right in a way that would satisfy a seventeenth-century audience for whom theological niceties might religiously, and even politically, mean life or death.

The consequences of this are widespread. The good characters cannot invent freely. They must always be wise and judicious, the reverse of histrionic. Their arguments must appeal to the mind by way of the moral sense, not by way of the emotions. They cannot clothe their words in suasive language without undermining the power of truth to stand in its own light, unaided by insidious stylistic devices. They cannot, above all, attempt to ally themselves on the sly with those 'weak and beggarly elements' in man's soul out of which tempters and devils make good capital. They have to be as innocent as the dove without being as cunning as the serpent.

As far as *Paradise Lost* is concerned, Milton had further serious obstacles in his path, and not least among them the often intractable nature of his myth. The tragic intensity of some of the speeches of Satan and Adam transcends and perhaps weakens the already precarious theological framework, for reasons which Milton, as a poet, could do little to control. But in *Comus* the framework of thought is less complex, and no hint of anything as serious as tragic feeling enters into the speeches of Comus himself. The lesser difficulties which I have just been considering still, however, apply, and have to be taken into account. I am taking now as a working rule that, in any of Milton's poems, whenever God, or an unfallen angel or spirit, or a character embodying Right Reason speaks, then he must be considered 'right' in this sense: that the religious and moral views which he expresses correspond to reality as Milton understood it, and are unequivocally to be accepted as 'true'. The good character is not partly right and partly wrong, and the truth does not lie somewhere (or even nowhere) between his views and views expressed by other characters. Likewise, when a devil or a fallen spirit, or an advocate of the passions against the Reason speaks, he is always warped in outlook and subtly wrong in every nuance and detail. His views, though intelligent, and embodying arguments which might in a slightly different context be valid, do not correspond to reality, and if heeded can produce only disastrous results. His whole concept of reality is out of touch with the facts and he is unable, quite literally, to say anything that is untouched by distortion.

In *Comus* the characters are surely grouped as follows. The Lady, as a wonderful piece of virtue, is right, and Comus, as a tempter, is wrong. The Attendant Spirit is a visitant from the purer regions far removed from our fallen earth and can therefore be taken as wholly reliable. The two brothers are ordinary mortals, but the Elder Brother in particular has understanding, and in many ways reiterates the Attendant Spirit's words. The Lady herself, touching her status, is both allegorical and real. She is Chastity (or Virtue) incarnate, and her purpose is to illustrate the immutable nature and wisdom of this state. She is not, like Eve, an entirely real person, likely to be overcome by temptation and ruin herself. But at the same time, because Milton thought that the attainment of virtue was not impossible to flesh and blood, she is not entirely allegorical. She is an attempt to portray an actual, if rather rarefied mortal, reacting properly to a dangerous and testing situation.

Our main difficulty springs, I imagine, from a sense that these two levels do not mesh properly when they are related to the dramatic action of the masque. The Elder Brother's insistence that his sister cannot be harmed seems optimistic as well as pompous if she is a real mortal lost in a wood. She may pass on, he says, 'with unblenched majesty' (l. 430), but we know that anyone, however virtuous, might be raped. The Lady's physical safety is also ambiguous in the rescue scene, when she has to be first recaptured from Comus, and then unthawed. This touch of melodrama injects action into an otherwise static spectacle, but the essential message is not really helped. We have to assume that the final victory of chastity is inward and spiritual, and that its depiction half-way between realism and allegory is the best that Milton the dramatist can do.

III

I hope now to show that this reading of *Comus* is the only one possible in the light of the action as a whole.

The first character to appear is the Attendant Spirit, whose opening words amount to presentation of credentials. He is one of those 'bright aerial Spirits' who live in a serene and calm peace, far removed from the corrupt world beneath the moon:

Before the starry threshold of Jove's court

My mansion is, where those immortal shapes
Of bright aerial Spirits live insphered
In regions mild of calm and serene air,
Above the smoke and stir of this dim spot
Which men call Earth . . . (ll. 1–6)

He has come, moreover, at personal inconvenience, to aid that
minority amongst mankind who seek to escape from their sordid
terrestrial prison and to climb to those purer heights where virtue
alone ('that golden key') can open the way to mortal flesh:

. . . some there be that by due steps aspire
To lay their just hands on that golden key
That opes the palace of Eternity:
To such my errand is, and but for such
I would not soil these pure ambrosial weeds
With the rank vapours of this sin-worn mold. (ll. 12–17)

The phrasing is Platonic, and Platonic thinking is at the root of all
Milton's theology, deeper than his humanism, his fundamental-
ism or his Puritanism. Behind these opening words of the Spirit
is the belief that Virtue is Knowledge, and that an unclouded
understanding is both the condition of virtue and its reward.
Temptation, in Milton, always begins with an attempt to cloud
the understanding as a prelude to perverting the will. In *Paradise
Lost*, for instance, Satan first leads his own mind astray with false
arguments arising from pride, and then he rebels against God.
Adam and Eve are later subjected to a similar (though more complex and accessible) onslaught upon their understandings, with
the result that they too fall from grace. The actual sin which
Adam and Eve commit is disobedience: they assert their supposed
right to ignore the dictates of God. The result of their sin, theo-
logically, is death – a permanent separation from God brought
about by a freely chosen and irrevocable action. The result of
their sin in practical terms (and this is the result of Satan's sin
also) is that their Reason is overthrown, and lawless passions are
unleashed which will bring their whole being – body, mind and
spirit – into degradation, disintegration and decay. Their minds
are no longer illuminated with insight, but move in a maze of
unfounded illusions and impossible hopes. Their spirits are tormented with uncontrollable passions (in Satan, envy and bitterness, in Adam and Eve, lust). Their bodies are mirrors of the

troubled souls within, and begin soon to show, visibly and unmistakably, signs of the hell that rages there. Of Satan, as he is shaken with envy, Milton records the following:

> Thus while he spake, each passion dimmed his face
> Thrice changed with pale, ire, envy, and despair,
> Which marred his borrowed visage, and betrayed
> Him counterfeit, if any eye beheld.
> For heav'nly minds from such distempers foul
> Are ever clear . . .
>
> *Paradise Lost* IV 114–19

And it is at this moment in the poem that Uriel, whom Satan has recently deceived, catches sight of the fallen angel's face and knows him for what he is. Adam and Eve, after they recover from their bout of lust, also see in one another's bodies the evident marks of a fall from grace:

> Our wonted ornaments now soiled and stained,
> And in our faces evident the signs
> Of foul concupiscence . . .
>
> *Paradise Lost* IX 1076–8

The loss of Virtue then is followed by loss of self-control and by growing conformity with a fallen world. This condition can be mended only by a gradual purification and discipline of the soul, undertaken in the desire to transcend this corrupt and transient world, and to seek reunion with the spiritual and intellectual realities beyond.

This of course is public doctrine, and one aspect only, though a central one, of the familiar medieval synthesis of Christian and Platonic ideas. The doctrine is central to the meaning of *Paradise Lost*, and it is implied, with the platonic elements predominating, in the Spirit's opening speech in *Comus*. When the Spirit speaks of an ascent 'by due steps' to the eternal world, he is thinking in terms of the Platonic ladder of love, with the meaning adapted to a Christian context. His first words, therefore, give a clear indication of the masque's world of ideas, and he goes on without a pause to say that he has come to protect the Lady, who is wandering in the allegorical wood of human perplexities, from an enemy who is planning to tempt her there. This account of the situation at once removes what follows from the level of a debate, and fixes the Lady as true and her enemy as false. The Spirit goes on to talk of Comus, and now not only the masque's ideas, but its symbolism also, is employed to reinforce Milton's main intention. Comus is the son of Circe, and nothing could be clearer (as Dr Tillyard pointed out) than the allegorical significance attaching to his enchanted cup:

> Whoever tasted, lost his upright shape,
> And downward fell into a groveling swine ... (ll. 52–3)

The victims of the cup are those who are degraded by unbridled sensuality to the status of beasts. They are travelling down the ladder of creation towards the brutes instead of upwards towards the angels. Participation in animal pleasures has so blinded their minds, that they mistake their degradation for enlightenment and their wretched and godless state for the best of all possible worlds:

> Soon as the potion works, their human count'nance,
> Th' express resemblance of the gods, is changed
> Into some brutish form of wolf, or bear,
> Or ounce, or tiger, hog, or bearded goat,
> All other parts remaining as they were;
> And they, so perfect is their misery,
> Not once perceive their foul disfigurement,
> But boast themselves more comely than before
> And all their friends, and native home forget
> To roll with pleasure in a sensual sty. (ll. 68–77)

The Spirit's Introduction helps us, therefore, to get our bearings; and it is followed by the stage direction:

> Comus enters with a charming-rod in one hand, his glass in the other; with him a rout of monsters headed like sundry sorts of wild beasts, but otherwise like men and women, their apparel glistering. They come in making a riotous and unruly noise, with torches in their hands.

We note (and at a performance, no one could miss it) the 'riotous and unruly noise', symbolising chaos, sin, disharmony. The Lady, in contrast, is always associated with music and concord, and her singing ravishes all who hear it with delight. This is one of the several ways in which Milton involves the claim of Comus to 'imitate the starry choir' in a sustained irony, and keeps the true perspectives clear.

Comus opens with some gay and infectious verse, in the manner of 'L'Allegro'. The idealised picture which he presents of pagan joy as immediately attractive, as it is intended to be. Is it a relief to hear the tiresome virtues discredited? – 'Rigor', 'Advice', 'Strict Age' and 'sour Severity'. (The unobtrusive but effective use of suasive adjectives is a routine piece of trickery.) But Comus goes on without a pause to make a claim which directly contradicts the view of the situation presented by the Spirit, yet one which the Spirit's words have warned us to expect:

> We that are of purer fire
> Imitate the starry quire,
> Who in their nightly watchful spheres
> Lead in swift round the months and years . . . (ll. 111–14)

He asserts, in fact, that the discords emanating from his rout are indistinguishable from the celestial harmony. Dr Tillyard noted this claim and called it 'impudence', but failed to integrate its far-reaching implications with his reading of the poem as a whole. In fact Comus is illustrating the type of blindness which the Spirit has just been alluding to:

> And they, so perfect is their misery,
> Not once perceive their foul disfigurement,
> But boast themselves more comely than before . . . (ll. 73–5)

He is involved in the doom of nonsense.

Comus now hears the Lady in the woods and resolves to tempt her. He explains, with the directness and reliability of a pre-Shakespearean soliloquy, his procedure:

> I, under fair pretense of friendly ends,
> And well-placed words of glozing courtesy
> Baited with reasons not unplausible,
> Wind me into the easy-hearted man,
> And hug him into snares. (ll. 160–4)

This should be more of a warning than it is to the easy-hearted critics whom Comus has also hugged into snares. Since the tempter warns that he is going to be plausible but deadly, we can reject out of hand any suspicion that the Lady should have taken just one moderate sip to prove herself normal. Upon her power to give the correct answer to Comus's 'reasons not unplausible' depends the whole of Milton's vision of reality.

The Lady enters, meditating her predicament in rich and moving verse. Those who complain that she has the worst of the poetry do not sufficiently consider this speech. Even on the naïve assumption that the more sensuous the verse the more worthwhile it is, this speech is among the finest in the poem. The Lady calmly reviews the dangers surrounding her, and is confident that a moral and religious armour will protect her from even the worst assaults of the enemy:

> O welcome, pure-eyed Faith, white-handed Hope,
> Thou hovering angel girt with golden wings,
> And thou unblemished form of Chastity . . . (ll. 213–15)

These, except that Chastity replaces Charity, are the theological virtues, and the reference to them reinforces the allegorical structure of the action. The assertion is not that the body itself can be protected from violation or destruction, but that there is final protection for the virtuous soul. Kenneth Muir has based upon the replacement of Charity by Chastity his belief that the Lady's virtue is criticised in the poem.[1] But the replacement seems to me fully natural in the circumstances, and I agree with Professor Maxwell in finding Muir's arguments unconvincing. Chastity is, in fact, Virtue, given the context – and in Platonic terms a key virtue, because the essence of purity itself. The Lady is putting on, in Pauline language, the whole armour of God, and inheriting the protection marvellously defined in Psalm 91:

> Whoso dwelleth under the defence of the most High: shall abide under the shadow of the Almighty.
> I will say unto the Lord, Thou art my hope, and my strong hold: my God, in him will I trust.
> For he shall deliver thee from the snare of the hunter: and from the noisome pestilence.
> He shall defend thee under his wings, and thou shalt be safe under his feathers: his faithfulness and truth shall be thy shield and buckler.
> Thou shalt not be afraid for any terror by night: nor for the arrow that flieth by day;
> For the pestilence that walketh in darkness: nor for the sickness that destroyeth in the noonday.

[1] 'Three Hundred Years of Milton's Poems', in *Penguin New Writing*, no. 24 (Penguin Books, 1945).

A thousand shall fall beside thee, and ten thousand at thy
right hand: but it shall not come nigh thee.

Yea, with thine eyes shalt thou behold: and see the reward
of the ungodly.

(Coverdale translation)

The Lady now breaks into song, to the excellence and harmony of which Comus himself bears ecstatic witness.

Can any mortal mixture of earth's mold
Breath such divine enchanting ravishment?
Sure something holy lodges in that breast,
And with these raptures moves the vocal air
To testify his hidden residence . . . (ll. 244–8)

This is the tradition of evil's irreducible tribute to good evidenced (for instance) in Iago's words about Cassio, 'He hath
a daily beauty in his life / That makes me ugly', and – of course –
in Satan's first tormented celebration of Adam and Eve (*Paradise
Lost* iv 358–92). Comus bears witness also to the Lady's serenity
and peace of mind: the evidence of a spiritual wholeness which he
cannot really understand, and is able only to destroy:

. . . such a sacred and home-felt delight,
Such sober certainty of waking bliss,
I never heard till now. (ll. 262–4)

The first stage of Comus's attack on the Lady now occurs, and
meets with success in that she believes his words and entrusts herself to his guidance. She is deceived, of course, only on a matter
of fact, not culpably. The insinuating and courtly overtones in
his speech ('And left your fair side all unguarded, Lady?') have
made no impression upon her innocent mind, and she has accepted him on his own showing as a simple shepherd. She is in his
power therefore, but only physically so.

The scene shifts to her two brothers, who are disturbed when
they reflect upon the possible plight of their mislaid sister, but are
enabled by the allegorical nature of the danger to pause for a discussion of its moral implications instead of rushing off at once to
look for her. This section is intellectually concentrated, and to try
to adjudicate between Comus and the Lady without giving great
weight to it is surely to miss the point.

The Elder Brother sings the praise of Virtue, and insists that no harm can befall those who are protected by their purity. The inner nature of a man, the heaven or hell which he has made for himself within, cannot be changed by any danger or influence from without. Only an act of free will can effect such a change, not the mere exigencies of environment or outside suggestion:

> He that has light within his own clear breast
> May sit i' th' center and enjoy bright day,
> But he that hides a dark soul and foul thoughts
> Benighted walks under the mid-day sun;
> Himself is his own dungeon. (ll. 381–5)

This looks forward to one of the important themes in *Paradise Lost* upon which I have already touched; that hell, although for allegorical purposes it is given a local habitation, is more essentially a state of mind – or, more accurately perhaps, a gradual disintegration of mind, body and spirit following upon an initial act of disobedience towards God. When Satan has left the physical hell far behind, he is in no whit released from the reality which its monstrous and shifting images symbolise:

> . . . horror and doubt distract
> His troubled thoughts, and far from the bottom stir
> The hell within him, for within him hell
> He brings, and round about him, nor from hell
> One step no more than from himself can fly
> By change of place.
>
> *Paradise Lost* IV 18–23

In a similar way, a good man can walk among any evil things without being touched by them. As John Smith, the Cambridge Platonist, said, Heaven is first a temper of mind, and then a place. This is the theme which the Elder Brother goes on to speak about when he reviews his sister's defences. The powers of Chastity are absolutely invincible: and, even if they may have to be compared with the 'snaky-headed Gorgon shield' (l. 447) and spoken of, somewhat dauntingly, as 'rigid looks of chaste austerity', the underlying beauty is not in doubt:

> So dear to Heav'n is saintly chastity
> That when a soul is found sincerely so,
> A thousand liveried angels lackey her,
> Driving far off each thing of sin and guilt,
> And in clear dream and solemn vision

Tell her of things that no gross ear can hear,
Till oft converse with heav'nly habitants
Begin to cast a beam on th' outward shape,
The unpolluted temple of the mind,
And turns it by degrees to the soul's essence,
Till all be made immortal. (ll. 453–63)

As I suggested earlier, Chastity here is only one example, though the supreme one, of self-control, Reason, and the life of grace. It is the entrance to that world of spiritual realities from which Comus and his crew are totally excluded. The Elder Brother goes on to paint the world in which Comus and his followers move:

                    . . . But when lust,
By unchaste looks, loose gestures, and foul talk,
But most by lewd and lavish act of sin,
Lets in defilement to the inward parts,
The soul grows clotted by contagion,
Imbodies and imbrutes, till she quite lose
The divine property of her first being.
Such are those thick and gloomy shadows damp
Oft seen in charnel vaults and sepulchres
Lingering, and sitting by a new-made grave,
As loth to leave the body that it loved,
And linked itself by carnal sensuality
To a degenerate and degraded state. (ll. 463–75)

This passage sums up many of the themes I have been dealing with and, properly considered, makes nonsense of the notion that the Lady is partly wrong. The Younger Brother is so impressed that he exclaims 'How charming is divine philosophy!' (l. 476); and the Attendant Spirit arrives a few moments later to say most of it over again, with his special authority as a good angel:

Within the navel of this hideous wood,
Immured in cypress shades, a sorcerer dwells,
Of Bacchus and of Circe born, great Comus,
Deep skilled in all his mother's witcheries,
And here to every thirsty wanderer
By sly enticement gives his baneful cup,
With many murmurs mixed, whose pleasing poison
The visage quite transforms of him that drinks,
And the inglorious likeness of a beast

Fixes instead, unmoulding reason's mintage
Charactered in the face. (ll. 520–30)

This is the clearest statement in *Comus* of the belief, already
mentioned in connection with *Paradise Lost*, that the body is an
outward and visible sign of inward and spiritual states. The
Spirit then tells of how he has heard the Lady in the wood, using
imagery which once more compares the melodiousness of her
singing with the dissonance of her enemy:

> The wonted roar was up amidst the woods,
> And filled the air with barbarous dissonance,
> At which I ceased, and listened them a while,
> Till an unusual stop of sudden silence
> Gave respite to the drowsy frighted steeds
> That draw the litter of close-curtained Sleep.
> At last a soft and solemn-breathing sound
> Rose like a steam of rich distilled perfumes,
> And stole upon the air, that even Silence
> Was took ere she was ware, and wished she might
> Deny her nature and be never more,
> Still to be so displaced. (ll. 549–60)

With Milton now almost ready for his central episode, the Elder
Brother finds time for a few further reflections, which serve as a
programme note to the scene to come:

> Virtue may be assailed, but never hurt,
> Surprised by unjust force, but not enthralled;
> Yea, even that which mischief meant most harm
> Shall in the happy trial prove most glory.
> But evil on itself shall back recoil,
> And mix no more with goodness, when at last,
> Gathered like scum, and settled to itself,
> It shall be in eternal restless change
> Self-fed and self-consumed; if this fail,
> The pillared firmament is rottenness,
> And earth's base built on stubble. (ll. 589–99)

This phrasing echoes passages which have already been quoted
from Milton's earlier poetry, and amounts to an impressive decla-
ration of faith. The ultimate value of life is said to depend upon
the certainty that Good is stronger than Evil, and that Good will
necessarily triumph at the last.

IV

The central scene is prefixed with the direction:

> The scene changes to a stately palace, set out with all manner
> of deliciousness: soft music, tables spread with all dainties.
> Comus appears with his rabble, and the Lady set in an
> enchanted chair, to whom he offers his glass, which she puts
> by, and goes about to rise.

Comus's first speech is a polished and luxurious statement of victory. He has the Lady as firmly 'in his power' as any villain in
Victorian melodrama, though only touching her physical captivity and on the level of allegory:

> Nay, lady, sit; if I but wave this wand,
> Your nerves are all chained up in alabaster,
> And you a statue, or as Daphne was,
> Root-bound, that fled Apollo. (ll. 659–62)

The Lady answers vigorously, claiming to be free in mind, despite the captivity of her body. And here we may allow that
though her manner seems ungracious, her position does not lend
itself to social charm. She is no ordinary maiden defending her
honour with greater or lesser enthusiasm, but the embodiment of
that vital and perennial conflict between chastity and lust. The
outstanding qualities of her answer to Comus are clarity of direction, precision of thought, rightness of moral content, firmness of
will. These qualities are set in balance against the sensuous, suasive and insidious style of Comus, and are dramatically fitting and
appropriate.

Comus now begins his first temptation, which is an invitation
to the Lady to escape from the toils, perplexities and hardships
of endless moral warfare, into the warm, refreshing easeful-
ness of surrender. The first half is a direct appeal to the sensual
appetites, which, as a human being, the Lady will be certain to
experience:

> . . . here be all the pleasures
> That fancy can beget on youthful thoughts,
> When the fresh blood grows lively . . . (ll. 668–70)

Then comes a call to surrender which combines Comus's supposed

concern for the Lady's happiness with the implied reproach that
she is being unnatural:

> Why should you be so cruel to yourself,
> And to those dainty limbs which Nature lent
> For gentle usage and soft delicacy? (ll. 679–81)

This is supported by the strong emotional enticement of the idea
that 'everybody does it' – an idea which is one of the strongest
weapons in any tempter's hands, and almost axiomatic in times of
decadence. Comus speaks of 'the unexempt condition/By which
all mortal frailty must subsist' (ll. 685–6), infusing great suasive
force into his placing of 'unexempt' and 'must', and follows with
the narcotic lotus-music of a 'dying-fall':

> Refreshment after toil, ease after pain,
> That have been tir'd all day without repast,
> And timely rest have wanted ... (ll. 687–9)

The Lady's reply is as sharp and unenchanting as a douche of
cold water, and exactly what is required by the drama. If we are
not ourselves victims of Comus's spells, and are responding to the
work as it exists in Milton's language, we shall be filled with relief and austere joy by what she has to say, and the way she has
to say it. She states, quite unequivocally, that Comus is wrong.
She sweeps away at one stroke the seductive and evil plausibility
of his tone. She looks at the mixed rabble who have heeded him in
the past, and sees them not as they are fallaciously represented to
be but as they are:

> ... What grim aspects are these,
> These ugly-headed monsters? (ll. 694–5)

This is to see things steadily and to see them whole. The Lady's
words mark the place where her victory becomes actually, as well
as theoretically, certain. With so unimpaired a view of the situation, she is unlikely to be impressed by anything further the tempter can say. When she goes on to tell him, in no unambiguous
terms, that

>   ... none
> But such as are good men can give good things,
> And that which is not good is not delicious
> To a well-governed and wise appetite ... (ll. 702–5)

we shall accuse her of being 'priggish' only if we totally ignore
the masque's meaning; and we shall accuse her of being 'un-
poetic' only if we have a very naïve view of the nature and
function of dramatic verse.

Comus enters now upon his main temptation, which makes explicit the view of reality behind his attitude. He develops the
claim that the whole of Nature is on his side and, drawing extensive and powerful analogies, provides a congenial primitivist
interpretation of her message to man. This great piece of diabolical advocacy, so daringly and consciously at odds with traditional
religion, is one of the classic statements of a Bacchic and hedo-
nistic reading of the created world. The stoics, and others who
preach temperance, are represented as soured, foolish, and out of
sympathy with Nature's express example of fertility and abun-
dance:

> Wherefore did Nature pour her bounties forth
> With such a full and unwithdrawing hand,
> Covering the earth with odors, fruits, and flocks,
> Thronging the seas with spawn innumerable,
> But all to please and sate the curious taste? (ll. 710–14)

Comus draws from his own reading of Nature the great lesson:

> . . . If all the world
> Should in a pet of temperance feed on pulse,
> Drink the clear stream, and nothing wear but frieze,
> Th' All-giver would be unthanked, would be unpraised . . .
> (ll. 720–3)

The entire tenor of the masque, as I have been attempting to
prove, is a demonstration of the falseness of this argument. Milton has been creating a dramatic and poetic context in which
this classic but misguided interpretation of Nature can be seen to
be not Reason, but Unreason 'Baited with reasons not unplausible'. We hold our breath as Comus sweeps on to his inevitable
conclusion, that the Lady should descend to bestiality, and so be
ruined. Only during the temptation of Eve in Book ix of
Paradise Lost, when our foreknowledge of what the outcome will
be adds unbearable irony to the situation, does Milton work up
greater tension in a temptation scene. The temptation of Christ
in *Paradise Regained* is a tamer (though not less interesting)

affair, which moves for the most part on an intellectual and un-emotional level, and is predestined to very certain failure. The temptation of Samson is nearer to this in type, but Samson's bitter disillusionment and almost paranoiac self-reproach do not allow Delilah much chance to be effective. Comus, however, even though he has met his match in the Lady, has all that is most fallen and pagan in men on his side, and is more likely to find sympathetic ears among uncritical hearers than any of the Mil-tonic enemies of man who come after him:

> Beauty is Nature's coin, must not be hoarded,
> But must be current... (ll. 739–40)

To this theme, so familiar in medieval and Elizabethan seduc-tion lyrics, is joined a force of argument that has run through human thinking at least since the 'fools' stigmatised in Ecclesias-ticus, and the earliest Greek hedonists:

> If you let slip time, like a neglected rose
> It withers on the stalk with languished head.
> Beauty is Nature's brag, and must be shown
> In courts, at feasts, and high solemnities... (ll. 743–6)

It is a relief, though no longer perhaps a surprise, to find the Lady still unmoved, and very vigorously in her right mind:

> I had not thought to have unlocked my lips
> In this unhallowed air, but that this juggler
> Would think to charm my judgment, as mine eyes,
> Obtruding false rules pranked in reason's garb (ll. 756–9)

Her verse has exactly the right qualities to offset that of Comus – short, decisive words, clear syntax, sharp diction, and firm struc-tural control. She proceeds to deliver a brief and reasoned defence of temperance, in words which confirm our earlier impression (ll. 321–6) that she is something of a leveller; and ends by reaffirm-ing the faith in which both the Attendant Spirit and the Elder Brother have placed their hope:

>   ... To him that dares
> Arm his profane tongue with contemptuous words
> Against the sun-clad power of Chastity,
> Fain would I something say, yet to what end?
> Thou hast nor ear nor soul to apprehend
> The sublime notion and high mystery

That must be uttered to unfold the sage
And serious doctrine of Virginity . . . (ll. 780–7)

In these lines she brings to an exalted climax the poetic power,
austere yet resonant, of her own consciousness, and the assertion
of two unalterable orders of existence between which no communication can pass. The worlds of Heaven and Hell have no meeting, since the false cannot understand, let alone contain, the true.
Comus is naturally on a slighter scale than *Paradise Lost*, but its
pastoral world is not without great power. The Lady, as Virtue
Triumphant, has a different and less melancholy role to fill than
that of Eve. When her victory is indisputably won, Comus admits in an aside:

She fables not. I feel that I do fear
Her words set off by some superior power . . . (ll. 800–1)

and his return to the attack:

            . . . Come, no more,
This is a mere moral babble . . . (ll. 806–7)

is half-hearted, and speedily terminated by the arrival of the rescue party. The victory is won, and the rest of the masque, as Dr
Tillyard remarked, is in the nature of a coda – an enchanting
pastoral close (for now that Virtue has triumphed, it can afford
its own enchantments), but not of sufficient significance to modify
events.

v

I began by saying that though I consider Chastity to be chiefly
important in *Comus* as an example of Virtue and Right Reason,
I do not think that Milton chose it in any arbitrary spirit. In the
Platonic scheme of things purification is an essential preparation
for insight. The aim of mankind must be to transcend material
and transient things, rising 'by due steps' to the world of pure
spirit. In this pilgrimage any earthly ties and affections may prove
a hindrance.

Later in his life, Milton came to terms with the more specifically Christian view (which Spenser expresses in *The Faerie
Queene*) that Marriage is an estate as honourable as Virginity, and
equally rooted in chastity, temperance and Reason. But in his
earlier work (and certainly before the 1637 insertion into the
Epilogue of *Comus*) I think that he regarded Virginity as superior

to Marriage, both because it is more in keeping with the ultimate Platonic aspiration, and because it is more capable of inspiring moral fervour. We have to remember the stern and exhilarating heights of idealism among which Milton strode in his youth, and the passionately uncompromising dicta which he found there: 'Virtue that wavers is not virtue, but vice revolted from itself, and after a while returning.' While Temperance and due respect for marriage might be sober conceptions, Virginity is always a shining ideal. Milton's appetite for wholeness was, on any showing, more robust than anything to which we are accustomed by modern literature. It is a most important aspect of his genius, and greatness of mind.

In my reading therefore the Lady is an exponent of Virginity in its absolute form. But whether or not she would have taken kindly to an honourable proposal, she stands for unswerving Virtue and for the life of Grace. Her victory is certainly a fitting spectacle for marriage festivities. She is totally vindicated in the complete masque.

This conclusion is at odds with that of Mr. Woodhouse, in the articles mentioned earlier, and perhaps I can return to these. Mr Woodhouse distinguishes four different virtues in the Lady's make-up – Temperance, Continence, Chastity and Virginity. He maintains that the first two of these belong to the order of Nature, the third to the orders of Nature and of Grace alike and the fourth to the order of Grace alone. Upon this division he bases an elaborate and often illuminating analysis of the work, which seems over-complicated, however, by arbitrary distinctions. If I am right, Nature and Grace do not need to be thought of as separate orders with a tendency to overlap, but as two different modes of cognising and responding to the human situation. The philosophy of Comus is that of the 'natural man' in the Pauline sense: he is wholly pagan in outlook, and 'knoweth not the things of God'. The Lady belongs to the world of Grace, and her entire attitude, even at points where it coincides with the beliefs of Stoics or other 'natural' philosophers, springs from a true and spiritual vision of reality. We should not make the mistake of thinking that she and Comus are arguing at any point in the masque on the same 'level', or that the arguments of one can be thought of as 'positive' and those of the other as 'negative'. The Lady's attitude is positive, and unified, and right; Comus's position is positive, and unified, and wrong. The differences between them are entirely fundamental, and the masque consists of a straight battle between the two which the Lady wins. As I have insisted, her victory is not merely personal. The whole nature of reality is at stake.

VI

But of course some problems remain. The obvious one is the Christian framework, which necessarily dooms Comus from the start. It is clear that though Comus is said to be 'Much like his father, but his mother more' (l. 57) and indeed to excel 'his mother at her mighty art' (l. 63), he makes less headway than they do, at least in this masque. No doubt he is less fortunate in his victim; but we must wonder how far his failure is a condition of the allegory, with its removal of the Lady from a world of real flesh and blood. In the strict sense, she is immune to the Bacchic arts, which are one of the many natural forces defeated by Grace. Though Comus can still deceive her eyes when he appears as a shepherd, he cannot impose Bacchic hallucinations on her mind. She sees his 'ugly-headed monsters' as they are, not as they are said to be; and berates him with the words:

> I had not thought to have unlocked my lips
> In this unhallowed air, but that this juggler
> Would think to charm my judgment, as mine eyes
> Obtruding false rules pranked in reason's garb. (ll. 756-9)

This means that the temptation cannot really work for the Lady; though the dramatic interest may still centre, of course, on the degree to which it can work for *us*. Certainly, Bacchus is more formidable in *The Bacchae* of Euripides, and in the great work to concern us later in these pages, Mann's *Death in Venice*. This may be due, however, to differences of artistry. Euripides and Mann are concerned with the triumph of Bacchus, and their art presents quintessential instances of that; Milton's concern is with Bacchus's defeat by the Christian God, and his Lady exists to demonstrate the blessings of Grace. As always, individual critics will differ in their reactions. For a Christian Platonist critic – such as the present one – it is possible to believe that Milton and Mann are both speaking of immutable truths.

3 The Last Enchantments:
Arnold's *The Scholar Gipsy*

Wandering between two worlds, one dead,
The other powerless to be born,
With nowhere yet to rest my head,
Like these, on earth, I wait forlorn.
Their faith, my tears, the world deride;
I come to shed them at their side.
                Stanzas from the Grande Chartreuse, ll. 85–90

I

The Scholar Gipsy is a far finer poem than Dr Leavis's assessment
in *The Common Pursuit* (p. 30) suggests. The phrases used there,
'weak confusion' and 'intellectual debility', seem an insult to the
poem we know. Confusion there may be, and even debility, but
these Arnold shared by and large with his age. I shall not claim
here that his work is as great as the other five to be dealt with, or
that Victorian agnosticism could, by its nature, produce the
highest art. But Arnold is not confused to the extent that Dr
Leavis suggests: he does not believe in his hero literally, or present him as a ready or even possible 'way out'. The elegiac tone
might be occasionally over-soft and self-indulgent, but it presents
a dilemma real and bitter enough to the agnostic mind.

We can be grateful then to Professor G. Wilson Knight for taking the poem more seriously, and writing on it in his stimulating
and highly personal way.[1] Mr Wilson Knight perceives that the
poem is unified in tone and mood, and that its complexities relate
to genuine ambivalence, not to slackness of art. He sees that the
scholar gipsy himself is an important symbol, and that the poem
is more than a quasi-historical lament.

When this is said, however, it must be added that the Wilson
Knight interpretation is too subjective to pass without a challenge,
especially since it turns on the view that the poet's wisdom, and
the poem's, may be two different things. In theory, there is much
truth in this; but it allows Mr Wilson Knight to attach his own
wisdom to the poem rather too readily, and at the expense of

[1] *Review of English Studies* (1955).

Arnold's intentions as they actually colour his art. It seems clear to me, in fact, that Mr Wilson Knight misreads the poem; so this account can be placed, as an alternative, alongside his.

Mr Wilson Knight points to the importance of oriental references in the two concluding stanzas of the poem, and tells us that 'we must accordingly search within the main body of the poem for qualities roughly corresponding to the oriental powers symbolised by the Tyrian trader'. Such 'qualities' he finds in the scholar gipsy himself, and on the strength of them is soon identifying the gipsy with Dionysian powers (as against the Apollonian Oxford of the poem), and with intuitive wisdom (as against the cold touch of analytical intellect). The gipsy has an essentially undergraduate wisdom, an 'eternal immaturity' – and this distinguishes him from the dons, whose greater knowledge has made it hard for them to retain 'wisdom'. The gipsy exemplifies 'the essence of true learning; the opening of the mind, the wonder, the intuition of fields unexplored. That is why the presiding deity of a great university [and he is no less than this] may be felt as the eternal undergraduate.' The dons are lacking in his qualities, and need his energy and freshness to preserve them from complete desiccation. These dons are symbolised by the 'One' on the 'intellectual throne', in whom 'the essentially backward, devitalised, "realistic", thinking of the contemporary intellect is personified. The state indicated is unhealthy, nerveless, and guilty of self-pity.'

Now this is, admittedly, a possible point of view, and one from which a poem similar to *The Scholar Gipsy* could have been written. Had Blake, or Carlyle, or D. H. Lawrence had the handling of the material, it would no doubt have come out in some such way. But one wonders what the author of *Literature and Dogma* and *God and the Bible* would have had to comment on such a reading, and whether he would not have regarded the One on the 'intellectual throne' as superior to the scholar gipsy in insight and integrity, even though less well placed than the gipsy for the enjoyment of an 'eternal weekend' (Dr Leavis's phrase). My own contention is that Arnold never commits himself to the gipsy (as both Dr Leavis and Mr Wilson Knight assume), but remains aware of him throughout as an illusion. This is the reason why the poem is structurally stronger than Dr Leavis acknowledges, and more central to Arnold's thought that Professor Wilson Knight allows. As we turn to it, we pass away from the *Comus* world of exuberant idealism into the dim and twilit world of 'honest doubt'.

'Arnold's poem', says Mr Wilson Knight, 'confronts our western tradition with suggestions of a wisdom, lore, or magic of oriental affinities or origin.' And having said this, he assumes that the confrontation is almost entirely to the detriment of the western tradition – thereby stating his own view, but ignoring that which we know to have been Arnold's. He speaks also of 'the poem's total meaning, which strives, as its title *The Scholar Gipsy* as good as tells us, towards a fusion of two traditions, western and eastern'. But for my own part I fail to see how the title 'as good as tells us' any such thing, unless we are predisposed to read it in this way; and in view of Mr Wilson Knight's admission that Arnold himself might have been unaware of his poem's wisdom, it is hard to see how it could.

It might be truer to suggest that *The Scholar Gipsy* confronts the joyful illusions of an earlier age with the melancholy 'realism' of the nineteenth century, and that in this confrontation, with its complex emotional tensions, the really moving quality of the poem is to be found. Arnold was as aware of the difficulties of 'belief' as any Victorian, and as determined as George Eliot to live and think 'without opium'. Like the majority of his contemporaries, though somewhat ahead of most of them, he had heard the 'sea of faith' retreating with its 'melancholy, long withdrawing roar'. In *God and the Bible* he does not hesitate to analogise the gospel miracles to the tale of Cinderella – pleasing, emotionally comforting, but unhappily not true. And because they are not true, there can be no question of our continuing to believe them merely for our own comfort:

> The more we may have been helped to be faithful, humble and charitable by taking the truth of this story, and other stories equally legendary, for granted, the greater is our embarrassment, no doubt, at having to do without them. But we have to do without them none the less on that account.

Arnold shared with many nineteenth-century agnostics a disbelief in Christian and medieval thought forms, but he felt no easy contempt for everything that pre-scientific man had believed outside the context of 'Right Reason' and Lockeian empiricism. On the contrary, he recognised in the earlier culture a beauty, a joy, an emotional and moral value, that could be envied by his own perplexed and troubled age: envied, but not regained. The fact seemed to be (and 'fact', 'belief', 'truth' were much simpler concepts to the Victorians, we must remember, than they are often thought to be today) that these earlier ages were happier than the nineteenth century, but that they were also inaccessible to it; that they were capable of sustaining man in a more joyful and serene existence, but only at the cost of a certain 'want of intellectual seriousness' (nourished upon intellectual ignorance) that was no longer acceptable. The opening lines of an early poem by Yeats capture that wistful and 'High Serious' acceptance of disenchantment which is so characteristically Victorian:

The woods of Arcady are dead,
And over is their antique joy;
Of old the world on dreaming fed;
Grey truth is now her painted toy. . . .

Arnold, however, though regretting his losses, was a realist, and a prophet of the future. Behind his thought in *The Scholar Gipsy* there was, I fancy, a *Weltanschauung* not dissimilar to that of Comte. He saw the world as an evolving organism which, like a human being, had progressed through childhood and youth to maturity. The earlier 'explanations' of things, theological and metaphysical, had been those appropriate to immaturity – glad, carefree, invigorating, but not grounded in reality.

Our religion, parading evidences such as those on which the popular mind relies now; our philosophy, pluming itself on its reasonings about causation and finite and infinite being; what are they but the shadows and dreams and false shows of knowledge? The day will come when we shall wonder at ourselves for having trusted to them, for having taken them seriously.
('The Study of Poetry', *Essays in Criticism, Second Series*)

When the world at last came of age, it had had to put away childish things. And even if the long-awaited maturity did sometimes resemble a premature old age, with the Victorian *avant-garde* haggard under the burden of its own enlightenment, there was nothing that could be done to mend the situation. Can a man enter the second time into his mother's womb and be born? In

The Scholar Gipsy Arnold's attitude to the gipsy is closely analogous to that of an adult towards a child. He appreciates and even envies its innocence but realises that no return to such a state is possible for himself. The child loses its 'innocence' not by some act of sin, nor by a defect of intellect, but merely by gaining experience and developing into an adult. The realities of adult life turn out to be less agreeable, in many respects, than childish fantasies, but there can be no question of thinking them less true.

The gipsy, like a child, is the embodiment of a good lost, not of a good temporarily or culpably mislaid. When Arnold contrasts the gipsy's serenity with the disquiets and perplexities of his own age, he is not satirising the nineteenth century, or renouncing it, or criticising it, or suggesting a remedy. He is, rather, exploring its spiritual and emotional losses, and the stoic readjustment which these will entail.

Dr Leavis has written as though Arnold laid his head to sleep, and gave his heart a holiday. But Arnold's stoic acceptance of unpalatable realities is among the most impressive qualities of his best poems, and 'escapism' is not a charge we should bring against them. There is no need to insist upon the naked dignity of such statements as this:

> . . . the world which seems
> To lie before us like a land of dreams,
> So various, so beautiful, so new,
> Hath really neither joy, nor love, nor light,
> Nor certitude, nor peace, nor help for pain . . .
>
> *(Dover Beach*, ll. 30–4)

or as this:

> Not as their friend or child I speak,
> But as on some far northern strand,
> Thinking of his own gods, a Greek
> In pity and mournful awe might stand
> Before some fallen Runic stone –
> For both were faiths, and both are gone . . .
>
> *(Stanzas from the Grande Chartreuse*, ll. 79–84)

The diction and tone are their own best evidence of costly intellectual integrity. In his prose, Arnold tried hard to salvage from the Christian wreckage an 'Eternal-not-ourselves-that-makes-for righteousness'. But in his poetry there is sterner discipline of

self-knowledge, and the full extent of the Victorian agnostic predicament – a tragic predicament for men of Arnold's temperament – is embodied.

It was not for nothing that Arnold laid stress upon the gipsy's
magic art. At the Renaissance (if an old-fashioned use of this word
can be allowed) man set out on a search for temporal power.
Bacon, the prophet of the movement, looks forward not only to
Newton and Locke but also to the Industrial Revolution and to
the Victorian idea of 'progress'. In the sixteenth century science
and the magic were the two principal techniques for gaining
power. By the nineteenth century science had vindicated its
material usefulness with results; magic had failed to produce results and been discarded. Science, however, had proved to have a
sting in its tail, since the spiritual losses entailed by the acceptance
of empiricism as a total account of reality were becoming yearly
more apparent. Magic on the other hand could still, in fantasy, be
thought of as an ideal and unqualified means of power, even
though it was now known not to work. Science had become, in
alliance with Locke's epistemology, an enemy of religion and en-
chantment, the discoverer of a universe of death; magic could
still be identified with dreams of a richer life in a more satisfactory
universe, since its very failure liberated it for poetic use as

> an abstraction
> Remaining a perpetual possibility
> Only in a world of speculation.[1]

The scholar gipsy embodies, then, the optimistic but chimerical
hopes of an earlier age. He waits for 'the spark from Heaven to
fall' (st. 12), but he waits in vain: the spark does not fall, as the
nineteenth century has discovered for itself (st. 18–20) This realisation is in the rhythms and tone of the poem, which is reflec-
tive and melancholy in the elegiac mode, not filled with dynamic
hope. The gipsy is committed to a discredited art, and so exiled
from Oxford. In st. 8, when he looks down on the lighted city at
night, he looks not as a presiding deity but as a long-superseded
ghost from the past. His very nature forbids him to enter, since one
touch of Victorian realism would reveal him for the wraith he is
(st. 23). The situation is not unlike that of the young Jude gazing
eagerly towards the lights of that same city – not to Oxford itself,

---

[1] Borrowed from T. S. Eliot's *Burnt Norton.*

however, but to the ideal city which his childish dreams have superimposed. The scholar gipsy turns away from the real Oxford, and seeks his 'straw' in 'some sequester'd grange'. His place is with the primitive, the uncultured, the unintellectual. Only so can he survive at all, so late in history.

In *Literature and Dogma* and *God and the Bible* Arnold insists that he is writing not for those who are still happy with their Christian illusions (the Victorian version of 'simple faith'), but only for those highly serious few who still value the illusion whilst being unable honestly to accept them. The scholar gipsy would not have been one of the readers Arnold had in mind; he would have been one of the happier (though perhaps less honest) band who enjoyed the faith of earlier ages simply because they had not been intellectually awakened to reality in Oxford. The gipsy is essentially outside Oxford; and his exclusion, though it tells against the happiness of Oxford, tells even more against the acceptability of the gipsy.

A similar balance will be found in Arnold's well-known prose passage about Oxford. He expresses his love of the idealised city, 'steeped in sentiment as she lies, spreading her gardens to the moonlight, and whispering from her towers the last enchantments of the Middle Ages . . . unravaged by the fierce intellectual life of our century'. But this Oxford is a moonlit vision, a dream woven of those 'last enchantments' which Arnold was doing as much as anyone else to dispel. Arnold indeed was not unravaged by the fierce intellectual life of his century, nor did he expect the other inhabitants of Oxford to be. His moonlit Oxford, like the scholar gipsy, may still be as beautiful as a dream, and calling us to the ideal: but can an honest man build his life on dreams? The home of 'lost causes, and forsaken beliefs, and unpopular names, and impossible loyalties' remains an ideal to preserve us from becoming Philistines; but the causes are lost and the beliefs forsaken, the names unpopular and the loyalties impossible. In this Oxford, as in the idea of the scholar gipsy, the past tantalises us with its beauty and its hopes; but we know that for all that, the past is dead.

The Victorian predicament, in so far as Arnold represents it, was a tragic one, to desire with the heart what was rejected by the head, to need for the spirit what was excluded by the mind. For a similar complex of responses, we can compare Arnold's words about Newman in the Introduction to his American discourse on Emerson (1883):

> Oxford has more criticism now, more knowledge, more light;
> but such voices as those of our youth it has no longer. The
> name of Cardinal Newman is a great name to the imagination
> still; his genius and his style are still things of power. But he is
> over eighty years of age; he is in the Oratory at Birmingham;
> he has adopted, for the doubts and difficulties which beset
> men's minds today, a solution which, to speak frankly, is
> impossible.

It is this tradition in which *The Scholar Gipsy* stands, and which accounts for the power of it; the poem is not conceived, as Mr Wilson Knight would seek to persuade us, in that parallel tradition of Romantic or Christian or Social solutions to the impasse.

II

The first fourteen stanzas of the poem are on the whole the most memorable, and in these Arnold creates the myth of the gipsy. Analytical intellect is temporarily laid to sleep, but only in order that the myth may be evoked in its own strength to serve the organisation of the poem as a whole. There is a dreamlike quality in the verse, in the direct tradition of Keat's Odes, and an elegiac note deriving from 'Il Penseroso' and Gray's 'Elegy'. In the 'Ode to a Nightingale' Keats wills his entry into an ideal world ('Away, away, for I will fly thee') and re-creates the song of the nightingale as a symbol of eternal beauty. But though the vision is positive, it still belongs to poetry, not to life. The word 'forlorn' recalls the poet to reality, to the world

> Where beauty cannot keep her lustrous eyes,
> Nor new love pine at them beyond tomorrow.

The nightingale of the vision can reveal the bitterness of life in time, but cannot provide an escape; it belongs to art, not to life. ('The fancy cannot cheat so well / As she is famed to do, deceiving elf') The nightingale's song is vital and real as a symbol of what men desire, but has no reality beyond this. Similarly, Keats's Grecian Urn has a life and vitality which, since it belongs to art, is more enduring than the experience of men in time; but this is

attained only because it is not itself 'alive', and outside the
world of 'fancy' not relevant, therefore, to those who are. The
happy lovers will never despair or fade, but neither will they kiss.
The urn is a vision of fullness, but at the cost of being also 'Cold
pastoral'.

The scholar gipsy is similar in his symbolic function to the
nightingale's song and the Grecian urn. He is there to reveal the
predicament of man's place in time, the ironic gulf between what
man can dream of as possible and what he knows can possibly be.
Arnold is no more confused between fact and fiction than Keats
was, and to interpret the scholar gipsy as a 'programme' is the
most basic mistake about the poem that can be made. What
Arnold most wants to say to the scholar gipsy is: 'Stay young!
Smile like that. Never grow old. Never fade.' It is the impulse
that we also encounter in Strether's outburst to little Bilham: '. . .
don't forget that you're young – blessedly young; be glad of it . . .
live up to it. Live all you can' (*The Ambassadors*, chap. xi), or in
Pater's famous formula: 'To burn always with this hard, gemlike
flame, to maintain this ecstasy, is success in life' (*Studies in the
History of the Renaissance*). It is the impulse, I would judge, behind much of Arnold's love of Oxford. Perhaps it is what middle-
age always most wants to say to youth, in love.

The scholar gipsy is not chiefly therefore a symbol for action;
but his uselessness to the nineteenth century on the practical level
is always underlined. His associations are all with magic and with
the world before science; and as I have suggested, the choice of
such a figure was made by the poet for specific ends. The gipsy
is never seen in the poem by cultured men, or by the dons; he is
seen only by shepherds, children, maids dancing at night, simple
men bathing on a summer day, the housewife at work, and other
unsophisticated observers. It is the simplicity and 'faith' of these
observers which enables them to see the gipsy; but the One on the
intellectual throne does not see. (The non-readers of *Literature
and Dogma*, we might say, see, but not the readers of that work.)
The scholar gipsy has, then, the vividness and 'reality' of a child's
vision – which is the reality of fancy working upon a consciousness
alert and eager, but not the reality of anything apart from that.
In st. 1, the evening atmosphere is numinous; in st. 2, the 'bleat-
ings . . . distant cries' and so on are hypnotic, a summer evening's
trance, relaxed and contented. In st. 3, the poet himself retires to

a place apart, a bower sensuous and secluded where he can day-dream. In st. 4, Arnold submits, like the gipsy, to an escape – but still in the mood of an afternoon's diversion. The gipsy escaped because he was 'tired of knocking at Preferment's door', tired of competition, and of the battle of life. He wanted to change his civilised society for a 'natural' or 'wild' one, to change intellect for intuition, the head for the heart. His desire was to roam freely outside the paths of convention, to achieve an integrated life apart from the blight of Western culture.

He was, in fact, a primitivist, attempting to realise the myth of the noble savage, seeking eternal fulfilment in a world unoppressed by the pressure of civilisation, and hoping that Time itself, man's enemy, could be cheated.

But Arnold, of all men, knew a myth when he saw one. The agnostic who could equate Adam and Eve, and the Incarnation, with Cinderella, was not a man to be taken in by the Noble Savage, or to make such an elementary mistake about Time. His own ideal, as we know, was that of culture, and the scholar gipsy stands at the opposite pole to culture. The gipsy does not, we notice, have either the Hebraic or Hellenic virtues as Arnold understood them. He does not combine sweetness with light, but on the contrary, 'does what he likes', and does so in ignorance of the *Zeitgeist*. He belongs unmistakably to innocence, not to experience; to the youth of the world, not to its maturity. He is a creature of superstition and credulity: a kindly creature, not a dark one, it is true, but when all is said, Arnold's own sympathies were with knowledge.

In st. 8 the gipsy is seen on 'retir'd ground' – withdrawn from experience, like the 'youth to fortune and to fame unknown' of Gray's 'Elegy'. Then he is seen in 'a pensive dream'. In st. 9 he is part of an enchanted spring evening, in st. 10 he is a midsummer vision. The suggestion of hypnosis is again irresistible, and in the sequence 'river . . . bathing . . . gone' there is more than the hint of a mirage. In st. 11 the uneducated housewife sees him, in st. 12 the animal world. But through this sequence there is a subtle progression from Spring (st. 6), to Summer (st. 8–10), to Autumn (st. 12). Finally, in st. 13, we arrive at Winter, the season of deprivation and death. And it is here that Arnold himself encounters the gipsy. His vision is the Oxford vision; it is a vision of the gipsy battling through snow, rejected from the city, in difficulties, turning away from the city. The gipsy must 'fly our contact' for his safety. There can be no safety for *him* in a meeting with the agnostic intellectual who envies him.

In st. 16 the gipsy is again considered in his symbolic role. When contrasted with this symbol, the nineteenth-century losses are severe, but they are beyond remedy – Time and the *Zeitgeist* are in alliance against the gipsy. The opposite pole of the poem is the One on the intellectual throne, and this is the pole of course at which Arnold himself is. Romantics (including the Romantic within) may protest against a devitalised cosmos, but the Highly Serious will be constrained to accept. Despair, however, is not to be escaped, 'For none has hope like thine'; and patience, which is the Stoic virtue demanded of the disenchanted, is 'too close neighbour of despair'. In st. 20, therefore, the final truth emerges, not explicitly, but in the suggestions of the imagery. The reality of the scholar gipsy is *death*. He is in a place where there are no more doubts and joy is unclouded, but such a place is only to be equated with non-existence. In st. 14, Arnold has written:

> Two hundred years are flown . . .
>   And thou from earth art gone
> Long since, and in some quiet churchyard laid . . .

this being the stanza when he emerges from conscious daydreaming into waking life, before returning to his myth for the second, contemporary part of the poem. His recognition in this stanza of the gipsy's physical death is recalled by the imagery of st. 20 – though linked now with the added, and deeper, suggestion of his death as a symbol also: 'And every doubt long blown by time away. . . .' 'Blown by time away' can suggest only the dust of death – the death of a man ('Imperious Caesar, dead and turned to clay / Might stop a hole to keep the wind away'), and the death of an idea. Death is the gipsy's reality – for Arnold, at least, it is – and that is why the poet meets him in Winter, and meets him as a potential enemy.

And so the poem moves to its last major statement:

> But fly our paths, our feverish contact fly!
>   For strong the infection of our mental strife,
>   Which, though it gives no bliss, yet spoils for rest;
>   And we should win thee from thy own fair life,
>   Like us distracted, and like us unblest.

Soon, soon thy cheer would die,
Thy hopes grow timorous, and unfix'd thy powers,
And thy clear aims be cross and shifting made:
And then thy glad perennial youth would fade,
Fade, and grow old at last, and die like ours.

Reading this, the last word before the closing simile, it seems clear enough where Arnold himself, and the age he represented, stands. And, since the concreteness of the gipsy's symbolism is behind this stanza, to give precision both to the ideas and to the emotions, the poem in its totality realises, complexly and poignantly, the tragic impasse of Victorian unbelief.

In the final stanzas, the Tyrian Trader flees from the Greeks as the scholar gipsy flees before European culture. He flees from the bearers of 'culture' who will find no place for him in the world they are so light-heartedly inaugurating.

When Tennyson's head had assimilated honest doubts to the edge of scepticism, his 'heart stood up and answered "I have felt" '. When Strauss had undermined the historicity of the Bible, he tried to reinstate it as a myth. Matthew Arnold, also, tried to find an emotional cure for the loss of faith. In his case it took the form of an attempt to substitute culture and poetry for religion and to find a few axioms that could be made real on the moral pulses. But, when it came to the trial, his head gained the day, honesty won the victory over expediency. *The Scholar Gipsy* is a poem of unbelief. Arnold did not discover anything adequate to replace the hopes of the earlier world.

Mr Wilson Knight himself believes (I take it) in what the scholar gipsy symbolises, and finds in him a wisdom both complementary and superior to the 'knowledge' of Oxford. This is, naturally, a possible viewpoint to hold, but I believe that Arnold himself held an opposite one, and that the organisation of his poem is essentially part of the Arnold world. For this very reason, however, the poem is of particular interest to a modern Christian. It points, against its wishes perhaps, towards the abyss.

4 Murderous Innocence: James's *The Turn of the Screw*

... if he *were* innocent, what then on earth was *I*?
The Governess

I

Suppose that your secretary came to you with the story that two unusually innocent and angelic children were communing with ghosts and being corrupted by them; what would you do? Phone for a doctor. But suppose that a late Victorian tale, set in remote and romantic scenery and rehearsed at Christmas, offers this revelation? The intimations of evil, the portentous incipience, assume a different colouring. More likely you settle back, with relaxed good faith, to the horrors in store.

The basic trick in *The Turn of the Screw* is James's game with his genre, his choice of a particularly baffling 'window' for the tale. The House of Fiction, he tells us, has many windows, in which the landscape of reality is variously framed:

> The house of fiction has in short not one window, but a million – a number of possible windows not to be reckoned, rather; every one of which has been pierced, or is still pierceable, in its vast front, by the need of the individual vision and by the pressure of the individual will. These apertures, of dissimilar shape and size, hang so, all together, over the human scene that we might have expected of them a greater sameness of report than we find. They are but windows at the best, mere holes in a dead wall, disconnected, perched aloft; they are not hinged doors opening straight upon life. But they have this mark of their own that at each of them stands a figure with a pair of eyes, or at least with field-glass, which forms, again and again, for observation, a unique instrument, insuring to the person making use of it an impression distinct from every other. He and his neighbours are watching the same show, but one seeing more where the other sees less, on seeing black where the

other sees white, one seeing big where the other sees small,
one seeing coarse where the other sees fine. And so on, and
so on; there is fortunately no saying on what, for the particular
pair of eyes, the window may *not* open; 'fortunately' by
reason, precisely, of this incalculability of range. The
spreading field, the human scene, is the 'choice of subject';
the pierced aperture, either broad or balconied or slit-like and
low-browed, is the 'literary form'; but they are, singly or
together, as nothing without the posted presence of the watcher-
without, in other words, the consciousness of the artist
                              (Preface to *The Portrait of a Lady*)

From this justly celebrated passage, readers of *The Turn of the
Screw* can usefully equip themselves: with the hint that when
some see black others see white, when some see big others see
small, and James thinks this fortunate; with the reminder that
the artist's consciousness is everything to James and without this
there is 'nothing' (nothing of interest, presumably, to him or to
us). Thus equipped, we turn our eyes along the vast façade of the
House of Fiction, towards a wing where the windows are more
than usually bizarre. And there, framed in one of them, stands
our author, the most ornate pair of field-glasses at his eyes. But
entering the room at his invitation, and standing beside him, we
notice something for which we have not been prepared. As we
gaze on the strange and horrifying spectacle with growing con-
sternation, the face of our host seems obscurely amused. Is he perhaps warning us of some oddity in the window? Could the glass
be a distorting glass, or less plain than it looks?

And – to change the image – we approach this particular
story with the feeling that we are entering an unusually intricate
maze. It is a maze with a very baffling constructional feature, in
that several highly promising paths turn back on themselves just
when progress has been made. If we embark for instance on the
path of the 'straight' ghost story, we are guided personally along
it by the narrator, whose authority is assured, if palpitating, and
occasionally obscure. 'Are you quite sure this is the way?' we ask,
and 'Yes', she answers, 'I know! I know! I know!' 'But how do
you know?' we pursue, pausing a moment where the path
divides itself. '*She* knows, ask her!' returns the Governess,
pointing to the little girl, who is with her, trotting along, hugged
in a close embrace. Then, as we are about to take this advice, she

tops us: 'No, for God's sake *don't*; she'll lie!' So we go on following, momentarily lulled by this logic; but wishing that our guide didn't sound so much as though she were laughing or weeping (was that a suppressed howl?), and that she didn't look so dreadfully queer. The snag about this path is precisely our growing doubts about the guide's reliability, which she herself, although fitfully, seems to share. Her main fear even appears to be that we shall doubt her: that the path will turn suddenly, as it does now, leading us back to the exact point where we came in.

Shall we commit ourselves instead then to Mrs. Grose's guidance? She looks sane and commonsensical, and her path is encouragingly parallel to the first. She goes ahead of us, chattering pleasantly and expansively, glad to find we are real gentlemen (unlike some people), relieved that we have come properly dressed for the occasion in our hats. But within yards, the poor lady takes a turn she hardly expected; now she looks this way and that with wondering perplexity; now she is off again, but patently in circles. It also appears that she was relying upon *us* for the directions. A pity this didn't strike us before!

So, groping back to the start, we look for other possible directions. Should we take our bearings from the unfortunate childen, following their broad if murky path from heaven to hell? Yet they seem somehow remote from us, though clearly visible; they are trying to say something, but it is hard to hear them. Their very beauty acts on our senses as a distraction. They are leading us into a strangely unlighted part of the maze.

II

In these perplexities it may be useful to turn to some previous visitors, and to hear what they have to report. The *Casebook* on *The Turn of the Screw* assembles a fine cross-section of previous travellers, all full of conflicting stories of labyrinthine intricacies, all turning the screw as energetically and ingeniously as the delighted author could have wished.[1] The one thing no traveller joining their company can doubt is his peril: it is a sobering thought that the greatest of modern ironists should have hung over this

[1] Gerald Willen (ed.), *A Casebook on Henry James's 'The Turn of the Screw'* (Crowell, New York, 1960). All page references to the story itself, and to its critics, relate to this edition.

particular work his personal warning, 'an *amusette* to catch those not easily caught'. Less surprising than it might have been, then, to find the reports so widely differing, and the tempers of the reporters sometimes high. There are those who look through the window in the House of Fiction alongside the Governess, and see with her the angelic children ruined by spirits loose from hell. A clearer picture this, in outline than in the details; what are the children in fact doing with the ghosts? We can only speculate with the Governess on sickening possibilities, giving our own imagination as full a prerogative as she does hers. But other observers see a prospect different, if hardly less harrowing: a spectacle of two ordinary children helpless in the hands of a mad woman, and unable to find the formula of escape. And there are others who see in the spreading field two slightly odd children with real ghosts pursuing them, but who find the Governess herself the oddest and the most frightening actor in the scene. The Governess is *used* by the ghosts, on this viewing, in their plot against the children, much as Phaedra is used by Aphrodite in Euripides' play. And finally, there are those who give way to impatience at the complexities. Isn't the whole thing an elaborate hoax, a trap which critics would be well advised to avoid?

My main intention is to join in the debate on all of these problems, but I ought first to say where I stand. I take the tale to be a story of a mad Governess, a woman suffering from delusions, who imagines the ghosts, which have no existence except in her delusions, and who finally drives the little girl into fever and kills the little boy, either by frightening him unbearably, or more probably by throttling him in her embrace. I find myself in complete agreement with Professor Harold C. Goddard, whose work on *The Turn of the Screw* (pp. 244–72) was written as a lecture in 1920, though it was not published until 1957, when the debate was well under way:

> If on your first reading of *The Turn of the Screw* the hypothesis did not occur to you that the governess is insane, run through the story again and you will hardly know which to admire more, James's daring in introducing the cruder physical as distinguished from the subtler psychological symptoms of insanity, or his skill in covering them up and seeming to explain them away. The insane woman is telling her own story. She cannot see her own insanity – she can

only see its reflection, as it were, in the faces, trace its effect
on the acts, of others.

The evidence for this insanity is extensive, and numerous critics
have made out the case. All I want to do, before passing to my
own concerns, is to note certain confirmations not, to my knowledge, commented upon. The saga of what the Governess says, and
does, is one great puzzle; but the things she does not say and do
are scarcely less odd. What should a Governess do when a boy is
sent down from school with no explanation? Write to the Headmaster, to discover the reason; but this is not the Governess's way.
He's 'an injury to the others', she decides, and 'It can only have
one meaning'. (Mrs Grose wants to know what that meaning is,
but like us, she doesn't find out.) The Governess reflects later that
it is a blessing in disguise to have Miles at home with her, since,
irrespective of what he might have done at school and of the portentous new menaces gathering around him, he is 'only too fine
and fair for the horrid, unclean school-world'. She decides that
he has been maligned by the Headmaster, and has merely 'paid
the price' for being too good. But at the same time, the corruption in this angelic child is becoming apparent to her; she is already pressing Mrs Grose for news of the 'evils' he has done.
Clearly she thinks it has something to do with sex, but Mrs Grose
is not confirming this. Later, she discovers that he steals: he steals
her letter, it will be remembered, according to Mrs Grose's sus-
picions – though earlier we have heard that the letter was still in
the Governess's pocket, and Miles's 'confession' is extorted under
circumstances where he might well confess to anything or everything. (Salem has sometimes been invoked in explaining this tale.)
It is worth remembering, too, that the Governess herself has not
scrupled virtually to steal her charges' letters: 'I let my charges
understand that their own letters were but charming literary
exercises. They were too beautiful to be posted; I kept them myself; I have them all to this hour.'

One can take one's choice, then, about the manifestation of
Miles's evil; but the 'certitude' of it is extensively bandied about
by the Governess and Mrs Grose. The Governess's idea that Miles
is 'evil' is first fed by, the later uses, Mrs Grose's considerably
different admission that he is 'bad'. What Mrs Grose means by
'bad' is that he has consorted with people she disapproved of, including his former nursemaid Miss Jessel, and that he has been

mildly rude to her when she interfered (rude, however, in a manner especially wounding since snobbery is one of her weaker points). Mrs Grose is entirely explicit in her meaning, but the Governess doesn't heed this. She converts 'bad' into 'evil' without any midway stopping-place, relying on Mrs Grose's pleasurable thrill in flirting with the worst.

Then, later, Miles proves he is 'bad' by going out at night into the garden – he wants to prove he is a normal boy rather than an angel in the hope of being sent back to school. His most frightening encounters with the Governess are still in the future, but it cannot be pleasant to have her drifting round the house in her insomniac condition (in one of her encounters with Quint's ghost on the staircase she reveals that she has been awake, without fully realising it, until dawn), or to be hugged to her bosom with sobs and laughs. But again, 'bad' gets turned into 'evil', because the Governess sees him looking up at the tower, and she is absolutely certain, in her intuitive way, that Quint's ghost is revealed to him on the top.

All of this adds up to the fact that Miles is less 'angelic' than the Governess in her other moods thinks him, but it is slender proof that he is damned. Flora's evils, on the other hand, are still more tenuous. The first is her failure to see the ghost of Miss Jessel across the lake when the Governess sees it (and this despite the fact that she has her back to it! – a diabolical evidence of complicity, the Governess decides); the second is that when she has escaped for an hour from the Governess's terrifying presence, with Miles's gallant connivance, she turns out to be more scared of the pursuing Governess herself than of the Governess's ghosts. Even Mrs Grose is by now scared out of her complacency, since she cannot see the ghost either, and she at last suspects, no doubt, that the Governess is mad. But unfortunately Flora becomes delirious from shock and uses bad language; and Mrs Grose, who is too ignorant to know that this is normal in very ordinary and indeed virtuous people under delirium, sways back again half to the Governess's side.

The actual evidence of the children's wickedness seems then lacking; what we are shown, albeit obliquely, is their tribulations at the hands of their would-be saviour and her friend. But let us suppose for the moment that they really are wicked, and that the Governess is right to find in the very lack of evidence further proof of their diabolical ways. What is a Governess to do with such threatened charges? Obviously send for their Guardian, who is bound to be concerned about such exceptional dangers, however firmly he has asked to be left undisturbed. But the Governess fails to do this, on the grounds that he will think she is lying; that he will see she is in love with him (which she admits); that he will think she is mad. Here, one pauses to wonder how normal this is as a reaction. Do rich men in Harley Street normally expect their servants to fall in love with them, and do servants normally think this is what they expect? But this could be put down simply to an inexperienced young girl's romanticism, since she remembers her interview through a fairy-tale luminosity, and compares her situation explicitly with Jane Eyre's. None the less it is an odd set of reasons for withholding from him the terrible fate confronting the children, and her fear that she will be thought mad comes uncomfortably near the mark. It is also odd, when one thinks of it, that the children are never threatened with their Guardian; on the contrary, we see Miles, for all his supposed love of Bly and its corruptions, making several desperate and unsuccessful attempts to get in touch.

But allow again for argument, that the master is ruled out as a source of comfort; ought the Governess not to turn to the other servants for help? But she seems to have a slender grip on the reality of the other servants. There is the invaluable Mrs Grose, to be confided in and generally worked upon, but the rest of the household is spoken of with revealing vagueness throughout. At the beginning of the tale the staff is listed for us by Douglas: Mrs Grose herself, and 'further, a cook, a housemaid, a dairywoman, an old pony, an old groom, an old gardener'. When the Governess arrives she sees a 'pair of maids looking out' of an upstair window, but she is more impressed by her first encounter with her future confidante, 'a civil person who dropped me as decent a curtsey as if I had been the mistress or a distinguished visitor'. Once, she speaks of 'the half-dozen maids and men who were still of our small colony'; and on the Sunday morning when she thinks of flight, she reflects that she can get back to the house without being seen 'since so many of the servants will be in church'. (Later, she tells Mrs Grose that she returned on that occasion 'to meet a friend'. 'A friend – you? 'exclaims Mrs Grose. The Governess replies that she 'has a couple', with a laugh the tone of which we are left to infer.) Then towards the end, when Mrs Grose has gone off with Flora and the Governess is planning her last encounter with Miles, she records that the servants are all staring at her: 'The maids and the men looked blank; the effect of which on my nerves was an aggravation.' There is also now someone called Luke, who is cross-questioned by Mrs Grose about the supposedly missing letter. Miles tells the Governess that he has to go to see Luke – an entirely understandable attempt to get away from her, which she calls a vulgar lie. In all this, the servants hardly exist for the Governess except as people to be avoided, or to be suspected of playing tricks upon her (and this even though their 'respectability' has been stressed in Douglas's Preface to the verge of a joke). At no time either does this very religious woman think of consulting the priest. Indeed, it is she, not the children, who finds difficulty about entering a church.

The Governess's inactions constitute, then, one kind of oddity, to be pondered by anyone tempted to swallow her whole. Another oddity, connected with this but more positively sinister, is the mode of 'knowledge' that she claims. Certainly she has little ordinary Knowledge, little book-learning or sophistication; it is arguable that on this ground alone she is a highly dubious person for the children's Guardian to have engaged. Joseph J. Firebaugh has urged in a lively though eccentric little article that both Mrs Grose and the Governess are wholly ignorant, and that the tale is of two children destroyed by ignorance and fear ('Inadequacy in Eden: Knowledge in *The Turn of the Screw*', pp. 291–7). The Governess does not know enough even to act as a teacher; she admits herself to inadequacies, and this is doubtless one reason why Miles wants to go back to school. But allied to her scholastic defects is an ignorant morality; here Mr Firebaugh is on the same track as John Lydenberg, who in his article has this to say:

> Through her insistence on recognising only the extreme whites of Edenlike innocence and the extreme blacks of Quint and Jessel, and her refusal to accept the shaded greys that are necessary for any true *human* understanding and sympathy, she alienates the children so completely that they have no alternative but to go to the devil.

This is extremely suggestive, even if one disagrees with its conclusion; Firebaugh, however, goes further than Lydenberg, since he allows that Miles perhaps has been taught sexual habits by Quint and expelled from school for perpetuating them, but argues that this is nothing to fuss about; anyone as delightful as Miles would have had his sexual experiences with tenderness, and don't we all come to sex in the end? With this, I have some sympathy; it would be a poor look-out if all children unfortunate enough to be sexually corrupted or sexually precocious were to be pursued by ghosts, or by a demented governess, and destroyed. But I am by no means certain how far Henry James would have agreed; and certainly, if one does accept the corruption as a fact, the adult corrupters must be looked on with horror and fear. More importantly, however, I can see no evidence at all in the tale that either child has had any sexual experience or even knows about sex – merely evidence that the Governess is speculating on every exotic possibility to the top of her bent.

The real trouble with the Governess's 'knowledge' reaches, in fact, deeper; it is connected with the language in which she claims to 'know'. This is wholly the language of extreme religious fanaticism or of certifiable mania; she claims 'certitude' for her visions and her inductions, explaining the attitude of everyone else in one of two ways. Either they do not 'see' (like Mrs Grose and the servants) because they have not been chosen; or they do 'see', like Miles and Flora, but dissemble because they are fiends in disguise. It is worth looking at some of the passages where she speaks of her 'knowledge', and pondering how respectable on any showing, religious or secular, her claims can seem. Consider the occasion when she sees for the second time the vision of the man whom she encountered first on the tower, with a timeless period of wondering who he was:

> On the spot there came to me the added shock of a certitude that it was not for me he had come there. He had come for someone else.
> The flash of this knowledge – for it was knowledge in the midst of dread – produced in me the most extraordinary effect, started, as I stood there, a sudden vibration of duty and courage.

Then, a few pages later, she is talking to Mrs Grose:

> He was looking for someone else, you say – someone who was not you?'

'He was looking for little Miles.' A portentous clearness now possessed me. '*That's* whom he was looking for.'

'But how do you know?'

'I know, I know, I know!' My exaltation grew. 'And *you* know, my dear!'

She didn't deny this, but I required, I felt, not even so much telling as that.

A few pages later, she has constructed a system whereby she has been chosen to stand between the children and their dread pursuers: 'I was a screen – I was to stand before them. The more I saw, the less they would. I began to watch them in stifled suspense, a disguised excitement that might well, had it continued too long, have turned to something like madness.' Then, a page later, she tells how she becomes aware of the first appearance of Miss Jessel over the lake (this is the occasion when Flora fails to show any outward sign):

Suddenly, in the circumstances, I became aware that, on the other side . . . we had an interested spectator. The way this knowledge gathered in me was the strangest thing in the world. . . .

And when she gets back to the house, she recounts the episode in a slightly longer passage, that I must quote:

I got hold of Mrs Grose as soon after this as I could; and I can give no intelligible account of how I fought out the interval. Yet I still hear myself cry as I fairly threw myself into her arms: 'They *know* – it's too monstrous; they know, they know!'

'And what on earth – ?' I felt her incredulity as she held me.

'Why, all that *we* know – and heaven knows what else besides!'

Then, as she released me, I made it out to her, made it out perhaps only now with full coherency even to myself.

'Two hours ago, in the garden' – I could scarce articulate. 'Flora *saw*!'

Mrs Grose took it as she might have taken a blow in the stomach. 'She has told you?' she panted.

'Not a word – that's the horror. She kept it to herself! The child of eight, *that* child!' Unutterable still, for me, was the stupefaction of it.

Mrs Grose, of course, could only gape the wider. 'Then how do you know?'

'I was there – I saw with my eyes: saw that she was
perfectly aware!'

'Do you mean aware of *him?*'

'No – of *her.*' I was conscious as I spoke that I looked
prodigious things, for I got the slow reflection of them in my
companion's face.

Since this is the first Mrs Grose has heard of another ghost, there
is every reason why such prodigious things should turn her pale.
She continues, however, to probe the Governess's knowledge, with
the following result:

'Was she someone you've never seen?'

'Yes. But someone the child has. Someone *you* have.' Then,
to show how I had thought it all out: 'My predecessor – the
one who died.'

'Miss Jessel?'

'Miss Jessel. You don't believe me?' I pressed.

She turned right and left in her distress. 'How can you be sure?'

This drew from me, in the state of my nerves, a flash of
impatience. 'Then ask Flora – *she's* sure!' But I had no
sooner spoken than I caught myself up 'No, for God's sake,
don't! She'll say she isn't – she'll lie!'

Mrs Grose was not too bewildered instinctively to protest.
'Ah, how *can* you?'

'Because I'm clear. Flora doesn't want me to know.'

'It's only then to spare you.'

'No, no – there are depths, depths! The more I go over it,
the more I see in it, and the more I see in it the more I fear.
I don't know what I *don't* see – what I *don't* fear.'

From here to the end of the tale the Governess continues to assert her 'certitude', her 'knowledge in the midst of dread', but we
are never led any nearer to the grounds on which it can rest.
What we notice about her visions themselves, however, are certain textbook characteristics – characteristics sufficiently numinous to pass in a ghost story, yet pressing, if we once doubt the
genre, quite another way. When she sees her vision, time and
place are suspended; place becomes 'a solitude', and the 'great
question' of 'how long they have lasted' is one that can never be
solved. Everything is terribly still and heightened; there is some
hallucinated dislocation of normal life.

But added to the Governess's mode of knowing, there is her

concern with her knowledge; and this too deserves a closer look. The fear that she will be thought mad continually worries her; frequently she seems less concerned with the children's salvation, for all her obsessiveness, than with herself. When Mrs Grose comes in with the news that the delirious Flora is using bad language, her immediate response is 'Thank God!' 'Thank God?' echoes Mrs. Grose, aghast ('She sprang up again at this, drying her eyes with a groan'). 'It so justifies me!' the Governess adds, in explanation – an explanation at which the reader, too, might spare a groan. But this moment pales beside a later one, when the Governess pauses in the midst of her inquisition of Miles (he dies shortly after) to reflect with 'appalling alarm' on his possible innocence:

> I seemed to float not into clearness, but into a darker
> obscure, and within a minute there had come to me out of
> my very pity the appalling alarm of his being perhaps innocent.
> It was for the instant confounding and bottomless; for if he
> *were* innocent, what then on earth was *I*?

With this fine pair of reflections in mind, we might recall an earlier moment, when the Governess at last wrests out of Mrs Grose the idea which she has been energetically feeding into her, that Flora is being corrupted by the woman just as Miles is being corrupted by the man:

> It suited me too, I felt, only too well; by which I mean
> that it suited exactly the particularly deadly view I was in
> the very act of forbidding myself to entertain.

And we can also match with it, of course, the moment when Miss Jessel at last appears to the Governess while Mrs Grose is there to see:

> Miss Jessel stood before us on the opposite bank exactly as
> she had stood the other time, and I remember, strangely,
> as the first feeling now produced in me, my thrill of joy at
> having brought on a proof. She was there, and I was
> justified; she was there, and I was neither cruel nor mad.

As we know, Mrs Grose does not after all see Miss Jessel and justify the Governess; but this so little perturbs the Governess in retrospect that she wonders next day why Mrs Grose is so reluctant to go off, leaving her alone with Miles. And this, indeed seems to me a central clue to James's intentions; he is studying a particular intractable delusion, the nature of which is that, although its victim may be fitfully aware of the need for 'justification', there is no normal sense of how the outside world will respond. The Governess knows, for instance, that she looks 'queer' to Mrs Grose, but she seldom considers how she may look to Miles and Flora. Once or twice, of course, the thought does strike her: 'I used to wonder', she confesses, 'how my little charges could help guessing that I thought strange things about them.' And when she has her confrontation with Miles on the way to church, she records: 'I tried to laugh, and I seemed to see in the beautiful face with which he watched me how ugly and queer I looked.' But she does not link these insights with the actual causes of their growing tension; she is unaware that delusions produce in time the ambiance needed for their growth. The more the children evince signs of being evasive or of wanting to get away from her, the more certain she is that they are pining to be with their ghosts. When at last Flora cries out to Mrs Grose to be rescued, the Governess can hardly believe her ears:

'Take me away, take me away – oh, take me away
from *her*!'
'From *me*?' I panted.
'From you – from you!' she cried.

I know of few moments in literature more purely pathetic: we see at last the full agony of anxiety that has been growing in the children, as the Governess, 'like a gaoler, with an eye on the possible surprises and escapes', has allowed her delusions to grow and feed in their presence over the weeks. 'All roads lead to Rome', she has told us herself, 'and there were times when it might have struck us that almost every branch of study or subject of conversation started forbidden ground. Forbidden ground was the question of the return of the dead in general, and of whatever, in especial, might survive, for memory, of the friends little children had lost.'

The most remarkable single example, even so, of the power of a delusion to create its own ambiance, is acted out with the housekeeper; it is the scene when the Governess follows the ghost of Quint out of the house, on the second time that she sees it, and then re-enacts its frightening effects herself:

It was confusedly present to me that I ought to place
myself where he had stood. I did so; I applied my face
to the pane and looked, as he had looked, into
the room. As if, at this moment, to show me exactly what
his range had been, Mrs Grose, as I had done for himself
just before, came in from the hall. With this I had the full
image of a repetition of what had already occurred. She
saw me as I had seen my own visitant; she pulled
up short as I had done; I gave her something of the shock
that I had received. She turned white, and this made me
ask myself if I had blanched as much. She stared, in short,
and retreated on just *my* lines, and I knew she had then
passed out and come round to me and that I should
presently meet her. I remained where I was, and while
I waited I thought of more things than one. But there's
only one I take space to mention. I wondered why *she*
should be scared.

That final sentence is particularly masterly, even in this context – sufficient evidence, if more were needed, that the ambiguity
of *The Turn of the Screw* is not merely an ingenious game. My
own guess is that the Governess's delusions are schizophrenic,
though I would like to hear a professional psychiatrist on this.
What can be pointed to with confidence are paranoid symptoms,
which would no doubt be secondary: she thinks that at one point
Mrs Grose is in league with the children; she interprets Miles's
straightforward plea to be sent back to proper schooling as evidence that he has unearthed her secret 'fear', and that he in-
tends to 'use' this in a conscious plan for more 'freedom'. Above
all, she feels the malevolence of the spirits, the stare of Quint and
Jessel, probing the very depths of her soul.

III

I want now to turn to some of the critics who take other views of
The Turn of the Screw, and to those in particular who accept the
Governess's account. The most striking of these is Robert Heilman, who argues in '*The Turn of the Screw* as Poem' (pp. 174–
188) that the story is organised as a symbolist poem, and that it
is virtually an allegory of the Fall of Man. Bly becomes Eden, the
ghosts Satan, the children Adam and Eve; the Governess is priest
and saviour, sacrificing herself to expiate and redeem. Mr Heil-

man has performed the invaluable task of showing the extent to which religious imagery shapes and pervades the tale, and more particularly of showing how certain antitheses continually recur between angel and fiend, salvation and damnation, confession and silence, heaven and hell. The one flaw in his argument is that he accepts all this imagery as the embodiment of religious allegory, and fails to allow that every aspect of it originates with the Governess herself. He fails to distinguish between Christian images as part of the tale's aesthetic organisation, and the same images as moral meaning, allegorically conveyed. We have merely to make a slight adjustment therefore to receive an opposite picture; Heilman's article becomes one of the most powerful demonstrations yet that the Governess is mad. Nor can such an adjustment be in the least regarded as anti-Christian, for while it is respectable enough for a young girl to profess and live by religious doctrines, is it also respectable for her to cast herself in the role of Saviour? – or to assert her doctrines in the context of a claim, and a tone, such as this?

Before pursuing this all-important matter of tone and context, it is as well to mention certain other defences of the Governess that have been brought. One is that James's Governess cannot be mad because the case for defining this is 'Freudian', and James could not have known about Freud. This is illogical on several counts, the first of which (obviously) is that Freud did not invent delusions like the Governess's but analysed them; the condition has no doubt existed since the beginning of time. Perhaps this ought indeed to be too obvious to need saying, yet several critics in the *Casebook* pose very crude objections of the kind. Nathan Bryllion Fagin in 'Another Reading of *The Turn of the Screw*' (pp. 154–9) adds, for good measure, an intentionalist fallacy, in an attempted *reductio ad absurdum* that boomerangs with remarkable force.

> But by the same method it is possible to build up an excellent case for a Freudian interpretation of *Hamlet*, and surely that would not be reflective of Shakespeare's intention.

Another critic complains that the 'danger in the psycho-analytical method of criticism lies in the apparent plausibility'; protecting us from 'apparent plausibility' is hardly, however, a Jamesian concern. Yet another critic seems to assert that James could not conceivably have been interested in sexual abnormalities; and another, that no neurotic young lady could conceivably come from a country vicar's home. On such arguments, not much time is needed: but there are others akin to them which require further thought. Glenn A. Reed in 'Another Turn of James's *The Turn of the Screw*' (pp. 189-99) argues that the Governess does not sound mad in her narrative, and that no real lunatic could appear to be so calm:

> The clarity and logic of her record should convince
> any reader that at least at the time of the writing the governess
> was not suffering from an emotionally overburdened mind.

But this is not in accord with known observations; there is no reason to believe that delusions are incompatible with logic and clarity (rather the opposite), nor that emotional unbalance is always mirrored in literary style. The mark of a really massive delusion is that almost anything can be converted to confirm it, and that confirmation can be argued with every appearance of dispassionate good sense. When delusions are accompanied by hallucinations, there is still more reason, in the deluded person, for lucid confidence; the notion that a delusion must express itself in obvious unbalance is simply not true.

We now know, moreover, that Henry James had observed the symptoms of a somewhat similar neurosis in his sister Alice; and further (Oscar Cargill has unearthed this) that he might well have read in one of Freud's earliest published case histories (in Breuer and Freud, *Studien über Hysterie*, 1895) a case similar to his Governess's in *The Turn of the Screw*. We know, in short, that there could have been a direct influence of Freud upon James's ghost story; but do we need proof of any such influence to persuade us of James's insight into the human mind?

There is another kind of objection to the Freudian interpretation, however, which appears equally misguided, but which may come closer to true insight into the tale's success. This is the view that a 'psychological' explanation would rob the tale of its terror and diminish its stature; that it would make it 'merely' the story of a prematurely frustrated old maid. This 'merely' is from Van Doren, who said during a broadcast discussion of the tale (*Casebook*, pp. 160-70):

> . . . if the story were merely a clever piece of psychology,
> no reader, even a child, would feel in it the powerful
> presence of evil . . .

and again:

> She [The Governess] is no such creature as the story-
> teller makes his victim when he wants to deal in mere
> delusion. She is not ridiculous or trivial. As a matter of
> fact, she becomes tragic.

Is a deluded person 'merely' ridiculous and trivial when seen by a major writer? May she not be tragic as well? But this view is echoed by Robert Heilman (op cit.):

> Philip Rahv calls attempts to explain away the ghosts 'a
> fallacy of rationalism', and asserts, I think correctly, that
> the Freudian view narrows and conventionalises the
> story in a way that contradicts both James's intentions
> and artistic habits, and, I might add, our own sense that
> large matters are at stake.

Oliver Evans, in 'James's Air of Evil: *The Turn of the Screw*' (pp. 200–11), says:

> But to view the novel as an implied case history, a
> mere clinical record, is to deprive the reader of the
> peculiar sense of horror which it was James's ambition
> to arouse in him.

My first reaction to such remarks is to think them slick – and so, in tone, some of them are. The terror of the tale is attested by its imaginative hold over all its critics: no mere interpretation (to put 'mere' in its place) impoverishes this. The critics I have just quoted treat the idea of madness with remarkable complacence; the 'mad old maid' is surely a concept of everyday inattention, not of a creative genius writing at the height of his powers. It is indisputable too that Flora is driven to delirium and Miles to destruction; both children are terrifyingly exposed and menaced on any reading one cares to propound.

None the less the sense that some power of evil resides in the supernatural intimations, and that a purely clinical reading be-lies our reading experience, cannot be simply dismissed. It seems to me, rather, to point to something central, though I interpret the implications in a different way. The truth is that the Gover-ness's consciousness, whether sane or insane, is literally central; it is the story's imaginative power. The sick horror, the numinous dread, the presence of unutterable evil, are all made real in it, with the power of a consciousness roused and creative to the highest degree. This surely is why the story haunts us, and the narrator seems tragic; and why the ironic ambiguities, far from deflecting intensity, are just one further turn of the screw. The Governess is creative to a degree, in fact, which implicates her author; we scarcely know, in such a creation, where the one of them ends and the other begins. She even has some of the creative traits of her author: one is struck for instance by the manner in which her fantasy originates and grows. The man on the top of the tower is the true beginning of it – a 'germ', to use James's word from the prefaces, which finds prepared and creative soil. James himself protected his 'germs' from further prosaic knowledge, and encouraged them to grow by laws and impulses of their own. The Governess's sense of symmetry is also not unlike her creator's; her awareness of the 'suitability' of two corrupting ghosts, one for each of the children, might remind us of James himself in the Preface to *What Maisie Knew*:

> The wretched infant was thus to find itself practically disowned, rebounding from racquet to racquet like a tennis-ball or a shuttlecock. This figure could but touch the fancy to the quick and strike one as the beginning of a story – a story commanding a great choice of developments. I recollect, however, promptly thinking that for a proper symmetry the second parent should marry too – which in the case named to me indeed would probably soon occur, and was in any case what the ideal of the situation required. The second step-parent would have but to be correspondingly incommoded by obligations to the offspring of a hated predecessor for the misfortune of the little victim to become altogether exemplary.

The Governess's mode of 'knowing' resembles, moreover, the artist's mode of creating; it is, as the quotations in my previous section seem to demonstrate, her elaboration of what the ideal situation demands for itself; the ideal situation worked out, of course, in terms of her perceived mission as saviour, and the depth of her fear.

The similarities between madness and genius are notorious,

but the differences between them must also be of interest to a creative mind. May not the chief difference between them be in fact what James's Governess precisely exemplifies: the loss of a saving distinction in madness, between creative fantasy and objective truth? James of all men knew the perils of this fascinating territory; *The Sacred Fount* is a further exploration of the gulf between even the subtlest observation and conjecture, and a situation as it 'really is'. Throughout James's later work, creative imagination is variously dramatised, but *The Turn of the Screw*, if I am right, is his dramatisation of it at the furthest extreme. The Governess embodies creative imagination wholly adrift from any saving perspectives, yet wholly messianic. No wonder that as the horror at Bly ramifies and deepens, our hair tingles on the scalp. In this tale the central narrator who tries to shape reality is insane, and the making of art, of fiction, by a mind simultaneously unaware of both external reality and internal fantasy is seen as the profoundest of threats.

IV

All roads lead a critic back to James's ambiguities, just as they lead the Governess to her ghosts. It is time now to return to the tale's sheer virtuosity, and to see whether this impairs its validity as a serious work. Several critics are again on the warpath, with opposing oversimplifications. 'What happens to the "tragedy" if we think of the story simply as a careful trap . . . ?' asks Oliver Evans in 'James's Air of Evil: *The Turn of the Screw*' pp. 200–211), expounding, like other critics, this unreal dilemma: either it is a 'tragic' tale and there is no trickery, or there is trickery and we must echo James's own denigration, though without his amusement: 'a perfectly independent and irresponsible little fiction', a 'piece of ingenuity pure and simple, of cold artistic calculation, an *amusette* to catch those not easily caught'.

Akin to this suggested dilemma is a still odder one, proposed by Alexander E. Jones in 'Point of View in *The Turn of the Screw*' (pp. 298–318). Mr. Jones argues that a mad narrator would violate the rules of novel writing, and cannot be entertained on these grounds. He allows that a novel's narrator may be, and often is, unreliable, but insists that the extent of the unreliability must always be clear. The writer 'may not deceive the reader *permanently*: for the basic convention of first-person fiction is necessarily confidence in the narrator. Otherwise, how would we know whether Huck Finn really drifted down the Mississippi on a raft? After all, we have only the word of that inveterate liar himself. ... Therefore, unless James has violated the basic rules of his craft, the governess cannot be a pathological liar.'

The short answer to this is that it overlooks the one quality in a work of irony which is supremely important – a quality to which Mr Jones's own irony, 'that inveterate liar himself', is sufficient clue. We follow a major ironist, or attempt to follow him, by nuances and overtones: there are no absolute rules beyond the jurisdiction of tone. We know Huck Finn 'really' drifts down the Mississippi because he is honest; Huck's honesty, beyond anything he himself knows or would claim, is what the irony everywhere attests. But we know that our Governess in *The Turn of the Screw* is not honest; this also is clear from beginning to end. We hear her telling direct lies, quite without hesitation – as when she tells Mrs Grose of her encounter with Miss Jessel, for instance, and embroiders it with a conversation that we know has not taken place. This is not, of course, the direct lie of a crude kind of liar: possibly the conversation expresses ideas she has silently intuited, a central aspect of this mode of 'knowing' that she constantly claims. But it is a lie, and with dire implications; a reminder that like most of James's characters, though with a special dimension of strangeness, she eludes any test of 'reliable' or 'unreliable' by simple rules.

The unreliability of the narrator is not, however, the whole of the puzzle; James added to her narration mystifications of his own. The opening of *The Turn of the Screw* is a masterly piece of misdirection, a sleight-of-hand as elegant as anything in Swift. At the beginning of *Gulliver's Travels* we are led to identify ourselves with Gulliver, and only gradually find that his contemptuous view of the Lilliputians rebounds upon ourselves. In *The Turn of the Screw* it is the Governess to whom we are cosily persuaded to commit ourselves. She receives the highest character references from Douglas (dead before we read it, but patently scrupulous; in love with the Governess during some later manifestation of her career, but never married to her); and, more importantly, we are settled down, with exemplary attention to comfort, to hear a ghost story by the Christmas fire. By the time when we see that everything – everything without exception – is totally ambiguous, the spell of the narrator's consciousness already has us in thrall. Only then does the audacity of James's technique begin fully to dawn on us: the audacity which he later celebrated, indeed embroidered, in his Preface, with such bubbling and judiciously ill-concealed delight. But audacity, and exuberant delight in audacity, is the ironist's prerogative; it takes a very naïve reader, a reader who has never heard shall we say of Voltaire or Gibbon, to assert that the exuberant ironist cannot be in the highest degree serious as well.

It is the seriousness of *The Turn of the Screw* which makes it so fascinating, and raises its irony so far beyond a 'trick'. Like all great irony, it is an education of the reader, offering discoveries of relevance and power. The double meaning in the style is a reflection of experience; the overtones and nuances, the subtle deceptions, the enigmas of interpretation are of kinds that can meet us, often just as portentously, in everyday life. The Governess's worries are not in fact trivial, and not necessarily eccentric; children can be corrupted, innocence betrayed and degraded; we need insight, courage, commitment in a dangerous world. In the 1960s, the Moors murders acted as a reminder that horrors of corruption are possible, to a degree even beyond the Governess's apparent fear.

But where are the dangers in a case such as that of James's children? Is the moral seriousness of the Governess, her assured assumption of authority, a sufficient credential in itself? Nothing is more important in great moral crusades than a sense of proportion; the diagnosis must be reliable, the cure not worse than the disease. It is here that James's hints about the ghosts seem so interesting, in a passage from the Preface that has been as variously interpreted as everything else:

> Good ghosts, speaking by book, make poor subjects, and it was clear that from the first my hovering prowling blighting presences, my pair of abnormal agents, would have to depart altogether from the rules. They would be agents in fact; there would be laid on them the dire duty of causing the situation to reek with the air of Evil. . . .
> This is to say, I recognise again, that Peter Quint and Miss Jessel are not 'ghosts' at all, as we now know the ghost, but goblins, elves, imps, demons as loosely constructed as those of

the old trials for witchcraft; if not, more pleasingly, fairies of
the legendary order, wooing their victims forth to see them
dance under the moon.

The mention of witchcraft has been taken up by two of the con-
tributors to the *Casebook*, both of whom support the Governess's
case. Nathan Bryllion Fagin in 'Another Reading of *The Turn
of the Screw* (pp. 154–9) writes:

> The purposes for which Quint seeks to meet little Miles are the
> same old purposes for which the Devil met young Goodman
> Brown in the woods near Salem. And little Flora is another
> Beatrice Rappaccini, outwardly marvellously beautiful, but
> inwardly corrupted by the poison of evil.

This view underlines Robert Heilman's article (op. cit.)
and particularly his account of the Governess's role at the time of
Miles's death:

> The governess's priestly function is made still more explicit by
> the fact that she comes ultimately to act as confessor and to
> use every possible means to bring Miles to confession; the long
> final scene really takes place in the confessional, with the
> governess as priest endeavouring, by both word and gesture,
> to protect her charge against the evil force whose invasion has,
> with consummate irony, carried even there.

Precisely! The Salem children were also urged 'by every possible
means' to confession, and they too were purged of their evil
(which followed them 'with consummate irony' even into the
courtroom) only by death. It remains to ask where we stand ourselves in our interpretation of Salem, and where James for that
matter might be thought to have stood. Perhaps we agree that
there was an outburst of diabolical evil in Salem; that the Inquisi-
tors, men of courage and integrity, were fully justified; that the
horribly corrupted children had to be killed. This is a possible
view of the occurrence, but not the only view; it is not the view,
by and large, which the modern world has chosen to take. I find
it somewhat alarming that some critics can so whole-heartedly
endorse the Governess's moral authority; it is not unimportant
that Arthur Miller was moved in the early 1950s to write *The
Crucible*, and that saner perspectives upon Salem and its supernatural visitants were thereby restored. If the ghosts *are* Salem

ghosts, we ought to be cautious; if the Governess *is* Danforth, her victims need to be considered with peculiar care. Even a 'psychological' explanation of Salem does not cancel the horror; however we take it, evil visions proliferated, and the victims died. The importance of *The Turn of the Screw* is just in this continuing relevance to matters more important than that of one 'mere' spinster and her fate. And clearly James was very aware of this continuing relevance behind his teasing: it is not idly that he sets us pondering, with the horrified Governess, on the evils at Bly. What safeguard is there against such evils but eternal vigilance? – eternal vigilance towards all proper authority, all crusades for salvation, all destructiveness in its subtlest and most insidious disguise.

And who is a fit person to provide such vigilance? – not Mrs Grose, whoever else it may be. The mark of this little tale is its endless surprises, but even James might have read Glenn A. Reed (op. cit.) with a positive start:

> In a manner of speaking Mrs Grose is the testing ground for just how far the reader may be expected to go in accepting the tenuous evidence of the governess. To the degree that Mrs Grose accepts the evidence, so are we as readers to accept it.

James often ponders the qualities he would salute in an ideal reader, but they nowhere approximate to those with which he endows Mrs Grose. Good-natured and well-meaning she may be, but what values of intelligence does she possess? – complacent and silly, credulous and superstitious: subservient to any appointed authority, as long as it is respectable; rather proud, in a way wholly snobbish; sentimentally indulgent to the children as 'little angels', but inclined to impatience; illiterate and uneducated, so that she can neither write to her master nor read his letters; anxious to please at almost any price. James's central technique, I take it, was to see how far readers could be made to go with Mrs. Grose; his triumph, to see so many outstrip her on the way. His irony is concealed, with supreme art, until the moment we feel forced to depart from her. Then it shatters our self-confidence, like a vast and terrible alarm bell, reverberating through every sentence of the work.

V

I should like finally to turn to the two famous 'cruxes' in the novel, the first of which is the moment when Mrs. Grose is led to identify the Governess's ghost as Peter Quint. This is the episode on which Edmund Wilson's original essay stumbled, to the delight of its opponents and slightly to the confusion of himself. Several critics, including A. J. A. Waldock in 'Mr Edmund Wilson and *The Turn of the Screw*' (pp. 171–3), have rested their case on this crux – just as the Governess rests her case on it when Mrs Grose is tempted to doubt. The passage is too long to quote in full, but I will start at the point where Mrs Grose has asked, of the ghost, 'What is he like?'

'I've been dying to tell you. But he's like nobody.'
'Nobody?' she echoed.
'He has no hat.' Then seeing in her face that she already, in this, with a deeper dismay, found a touch of a picture, I quickly added stroke to stroke. 'He has red hair, very red, close-curling, and a pale face, long in shape, with straight, good features and little, rather queer whiskers that are as red as his hair. His eyebrows are, somehow, darker; they look particularly arched and as if they might move a good deal. His eyes are sharp, strange – awfully; but I only know clearly that they're rather small and very fixed. His mouth's wide, and his lips are thin, and except for his little whiskers he's quite clean-shaven. He gives me a sort of sense of looking like an actor'.
'An actor!' It was impossible to resemble one less, at least, than Mrs Grose at that moment.
'I've never seen one, but so I suppose them. He's tall, active, erect,' I continued, 'but never – no, never! – a gentleman.'
My companion's face had blanched as I went on; her round eyes started and her mild mouth gaped.
'A gentleman?' she gasped, confounded, stupefied: 'a gentleman *he*?'
'You know him then?'
She visibly tried to hold herself. 'But he *is* handsome?'
I saw the way to help her. 'Remarkably!'
'And dressed –?'
'In somebody's clothes. They're smart, but they're not his own.'

She broke into a breathless affirmative groan. 'They're the master's!'

I caught it up. 'You *do* know him?'

She faltered but a second. 'Quint!' she cried.

'Quint?'

'Peter Quint – his own man, his valet, when he was here!'

'When the master was?'

Gaping still, but meeting me, she pieced it all together. 'He never wore his hat, but he did wear – well, there were waistcoats missed! They were both here – last year. Then the master went, and Quint was alone.'

I followed, but halting a little. 'Alone?'

'Alone with *us*'. Then, as from a deeper depth, 'In charge,' she added.

'And what became of him?'

She hung fire so long that I was still more mystified. 'He went too,' she brought out at last.

'Went where?'

Her expression, at this, became extraordinary. 'God knows where! He died.'

'Died?' I almost shrieked.

She seemed fairly to square herself, plant herself more firmly to utter the wonder of it. 'Yes. Mr. Quint is dead'.

How, we naturally ask, could the governess have known all this, if she had not indeed seen Quint's ghost? And if we deny to ourselves as readers all possibility of inference and fail to read carefully, our bemusement will scarcely be less than that of Mrs Grose. The occasion of this exchange is important: the Governess has just had her second vision of Quint, and has capped this herself by scaring Mrs Grose. To her question 'Did I look very queer?' Mrs Grose has frankly answered, 'Dreadful'. The Governess says this is because she has been frightened, but Mrs Grose has also been frightened, and they are neither in the calmest state. The vital clue slips in, meanwhile, between this introduction, and the passage I have quoted; it is to John Silver's credit (pp. 239–43) that we now all see what it is.

Even without the vital clue, however, the passage is odd enough to give us pause. The Governess says her ghost was like 'nobody' – yet at the time of the first appearance her immediate thought was that it was the master: 'What arrested me on the spot – and with a shock much greater than any vision had allowed for – was the sense that my imagination had, in a flash, turned real.' After that, she had 'thought, with extraordinary quickness, of each person that he might have been and that he was not'. But now, she says he was like 'nobody' – nobody, presumably, that she had known.

Next, there is the strange detail about the hat, which impresses Mrs Grose, since hats are a great divider for her, as social snob, of the sheep from the goats. (Later, the Governess tells her that Miss Jessel's ghost is without a hat, though on the two occasions when she describes it, no hat is mentioned either way). On the first appearance of Quint's ghost the lack of the hat does, however, feature; indeed, it is the only feature of Quint, as he is now described for us, that the earlier accounts contain. The Governess has seen Quint twice, it will be remembered, once on the tower at twilight, and once outside the window, looking in. On each occasion she stresses that she has seen him with the utmost clarity, even though the first time was twilight and the second a dull Sunday afternoon. On the first occasion, we have seen, she tried to identify him – and here a distinct oddity presents itself: if the master is not also a red-haired and altogether idiosyncratic person, how could she have made such a mistake? But on the earlier occasions she has asserted her clarity of vision without any identifying description; the only solid fact that gets carried over into this later description is the lack of a hat.

We now progress to the second feature which so impresses the housekeeper – that the ghost is wearing stolen clothes. How does one decide whether a ghost's clothes are his own, or someone else's? Even the Governess's remarkable mechanism of 'certitude' must have been stretched at this point. Mrs Grose, however, accepts this detail without further questioning, since the mystery now has her firmly in its grip. Clearly, the description given of Quint is an accurate one; he must have looked as the Governess now describes him, even though nothing of this has been revealed to us before.

How, then, are we to account for this detailed description? The answer is breathtaking in its simple audacity: Mr Silver has pointed his finger at some especially innocent exchanges, slipped in a few moments before.

[Mrs Grose]: 'Was he a gentleman?'

I found I had no need to think. 'No!' She gazed in deeper wonder. 'No'.

'Then nobody about the place? Nobody from the village?'

'Nobody – nobody. I didn't tell you, but I made sure.'

She says she made sure! There, in all its magnificence, is the admission: a journey to the village, to check on strange men who might be prowling around upon the turrets, with all the possibilities of gossip contained in that. So the exact description of Peter Quint, complete with his stolen clothes, his rather queer whiskers, and his tarnished reputation need no longer surprise us; what will surprise us is the Governess's skill in presenting it, and her careful shriek of 'Died?' at the end. Quint's death is the one fact about him that she is certain to have discovered; indeed, a little later the actual details of his death are recorded, details which Mrs Grose has not (to our knowledge) passed on to her, but which our narrator all unthinkingly records.

The other main crux in *The Turn of the Screw* is in the final pages, when Miles appears to admit his secret communings with Quint. The mechanism of this has been so splendidly elucidated by Harold C. Goddard (op. cit.) that no more about it needs to be said.

It is a final pleasing irony that a tale intended by its author as a *locus classicus* of intelligent reading should have achieved great popularity, yet that its critics must still account themselves so many potential trophies of the *amusette*. I shall conclude, as many other critics have done, by enlisting the author, through a central passage in his Preface (and the italics are mine):

I recall for instance a reproach made me by a reader capable evidently, for the time, of some attention, but not quite capable of enough, who complained that I hadn't sufficiently 'characterised' my young woman engaged in her labyrinth; hadn't endowed her with signs and marks, features and humours, *hadn't in a word invited her to deal with her own mystery as well as with that of Peter Quint, Miss Jessel and the hapless children.* I remember well, whatever the absurdity of its now coming back to me, my reply to that criticism – *under which one's artistic, one's ironic heart shook for the instant almost to breaking.* 'You indulge in that stricture at your ease, and I don't mind confiding to you that – strange as it may appear! – one has to choose ever so delicately among one's difficulties, attaching one's self to the greatest, bearing hard on those and intelligently neglecting the others. If one attempts to tackle them all one is certain to deal completely with none; whereas the effectual dealing with a few casts a *blest golden haze* under cover of which, like wanton mocking goddesses in clouds, the others find prudent to retire. It was 'déjà très joli', in *The Turn of the Screw*, please believe, the general proposition of our young woman's keeping crystalline her record of so many intense anomalies and obscurities – *by which I don't of course mean her explanation of them, a different matter;* and I saw no way, I feebly grant (fighting, at the best too, periodically, for every grudged inch of my space) to exhibit her in relations other than those; *one of which, precisely, would have been her relation to her own nature.* We have surely as much of her own nature *as we can swallow* in watching it reflect her *anxieties* and *inductions.* It constitutes no little of a character indeed, in such conditions, for a young person, as she says 'privately bred', that she is able to make *her particular credible statement of such strange matters.* She has 'authority' *which is a good deal to have given her,* and I couldn't have arrived at so much had I clumsily tried for more.

5 The Stranger God: Mann's *Death in Venice*

'I stand between two worlds. I am at home in neither,
and I suffer in consequence.'

Tonio Kröger

I

'Among the knotted joints of a bamboo thicket the eyes of a crouching tiger gleamed – and he felt his heart throb with a longing inexplicable' (p. 10).[1] This sudden vision of tiger and swamp overtakes Aschenbach in a mood of tiredness. He is successful, honoured, supremely disciplined and self-disciplined, and nearing sixty. The temptation is to relax, but the vision is primitive. Prudently, he decides not to go 'all the way to the tigers', but to settle for 'three or four weeks of lotus-eating'; and there is still the illusion of simple choice. But his vision is already heightened and perhaps dislocated by the stirring of vague and formless impulses from the past. The wandering stranger whom he encounters near a mortuary chapel seems brutal, yet obscurely exciting, and somehow familiar (later, a similar figure turns up as strolling player in Venice). The chapel is an intense and rather nightmarish vision of peace.

In such symbols, we encounter the immediate ambiguities of 'freedom'. As the novel unfolds, Aschenbach's decisions become less clear-cut, more hazardous, more assimilated to intimations of an obscure divine plot. There is the choice of Venice, and of the rogue gondolier; the choice of escape from Venice; the destiny courted and gladly accepted in the end. With hindsight, we may see foreshadowed even in the first few pages that time when Aschenbach's highest and only freedom will be the pursuit of Tadzio through labyrinthine byways and canals. It seems that he exists to become, in James's phrase, the purest 'case', the extreme embodiment of logic mercifully rare in 'life'. For most of us, one supposes, there would have been an exit with or without trunks from Venice station, an ending with dimming memories of regret

---

[1] All quotations and page references are to the Penguin translation, by H. T. Lowe-Porter.

and relief. But Aschenbach is destined to conspire his own completeness, offering himself entirely and in the end almost freely to his fate. Is the final decision ever his to make? As he lingers over breakfast just long enough to create confusion around his departure, his fine powers of self-analysis are truly asleep. When the courted accident happens, he seizes it with a gladness wholly at odds with a lifetime's devotion to reason and will. Only later does he consciously realise what has kept him in Venice; and then, when the moment of decisive choice seems before him, we sense it as an endorsement, rather, of transactions already long in the past:

> He sat quite still, unseen at his high post, and looked within himself. His features were lively, he lifted his brows; a smile, alert, inquiring, vivid, widened his mouth. Then he raised his head, and with both hands, hanging limp over the chair-arms, he described a slow motion, palms outward, a lifting and turning movement, as though to indicate a wide embrace. It was a gesture of welcome, a calm and deliberate acceptance of what might come. (p. 46).

II

The experience closes around Aschenbach in stages. First, in the spirit of *Tonio Kröger* and of course, Plato's *Phaedrus*, he makes an artist's response to the boy. ' "Good, oh, very good indeed", thought Aschenbach, assuming the patronising air of a connoisseur to hide, as artists will, their ravishment over a masterpiece' (p. 35). There is at once concealment; and almost immediately 'another yearning, opposed to his art and perhaps for that very reason a lure, for the unorganised, the immeasurable, the eternal – in short, for nothingness. He whose preoccupation is with excellence longs fervently to find rest in perfection; and is not nothingness a form of perfection?' (p. 36). When a little later he remembers the son he has never had, he responds to the boy also as a father. The mystery of the boy's name possesses him, and when he confers 'Tadzio', making the best guess he can from the evidence, he tacitly appoints himself guardian to the boy:

> Indeed, it was almost as though he sat there to guard the youth's repose; occupied, of course, with his own affairs, yet alive to the presence of that noble human creature close at hand. And his heart was stirred, it felt a father's kindness:

such an emotion as the possessor of beauty can inspire in one
who has offered himself up in spirit to create beauty. (p. 39)

By the time of his attempted flight, Aschenbach has reached the
knowledge that he worships Tadzio, and he speaks a silent but
fervent benediction over the boy. Is this the moment when whatever is good in an impossible love is consummated, and can be
preserved only – given the freedom or grace required – by successful flight? Already, Aschenbach's subconscious has warned him;
but when the flight is aborted, at last he *feels* free. Quizzical and
poised, he accepts himself as Tadzio's lover, and the boy is now
fully baptised into a private world. From this moment, Aschenbach passes into the new experience that awaits him. Isolated
from his own past and from any possible future, he passes also
out of the range of effectual communication – whether with the
beloved, or with his fellow men, or with himself. At first, the
weather turns round, and a new spring arrives in Venice. But
too soon, the prevailing imagery of disease returns, with Aschenbach moving through the steps of his ballet in an increasingly
sultry, plague-ridden labyrinth of Venetian ways. Too late, he becomes aware that almost from the start, the idea of the boy's death
has given him pleasure.

'He is delicate, he is sickly', Aschenbach thought. 'He will
most likely not live to grow old.' He did not try to account
for the pleasure the idea gave him. (p. 40)

Only after further stages are the secret words spoken' I love you!'
– words not without their honour, says the narrator, even here,
(p. 59). By now he has no will to escape; and even as the horror
of the quality of his love and the impossibility of living without
it envelops him, he knows that this horror is better than happiness.
'He who is beside himself revolts at the idea of self-possession'
(p. 74); and while Aschenbach knows and suffers violation, he
exults too in the most teasing and tormenting of Platonic insights:
'the lover was nearer the divine than the beloved; for the god
was in the one but not in the other' (p. 52). In retrospect, it might
seem that all stages of choice have indeed been illusory, as
Aschenbach passes into the power of 'the stranger god'.

III

Before examining this Bacchic aspect more closely, we must note the marvellous developments in the tale of imagery and theme. Of all modern novelists, Mann was the most consciously and fruitfully indebted to Wagner. To list the many recurrences, developments, mutations of theme would be tedious; but a few establish themselves as motifs and control the structure. In the opening pages, life and death mingle in alternating visions of swamp and tiger. These in turn colour the still and disquieting mortuary chapel, where Aschenbach sees the uncouth man with a prominent Adam's apple who so powerfully impresses him:

> Yet whether the pilgrim air the stranger wore kindled his fantasy or whether some other physical or psychical influence came into play, he could not tell; but he felt the most surprising consciousness of a widening of inward barriers, a kind of vaulting unrest, a youthfully ardent thirst for distant scenes . . . (p. 9)

This encounter, again, is recalled when the stranger's near simulacrum, more fierce, derisory and depraved, turns up as strolling singer in plague-stricken Venice (pp. 65–70). The imagery of death is now pervasive; and in the next passage, Aschenbach at last learns what sickness arrived in Venice along with himself:

> For the past several years Asiatic cholera had shown a strong tendency to spread. Its source was the hot, moist swamps of the delta of the Ganges, where it bred in the mephitic air of the primeval island-jungle, among whose bamboo thickets the tiger crouches, where life of every sort flourishes in rankest abundance, and only man avoids the spot. (p. 71)

From here, we move to Aschenbach's fearful dream, when the stranger god lurking behind these images and visitations is revealed. It is as if the figures surrounding Aschenbach's adventure might all have been phantoms, emanating from the god into whose hands he falls.

The sense of surrounding presences is further enhanced by the rogue gondolier who rows Aschenbach to the Lido against his explicit orders, yet in accordance with his unspoken desires and eventually – as Aschenbach discovers the impossibility of effectual protest – with his tacit consent. ' "I am a good rower, signore" ',

says the gondolier, ' "and will row you well".' When Aschenbach arrives at the Lido it is to fall into a deep sleep, from which
he is never to awake again to his normal world. The gondolier is
no doubt Charon, ferrying his prey; he is also a type of that other
gondolier who will later help Aschenbach to pursue his beloved
through Venice, and leer his complicity with the sickened man.
To these figures must be added the grotesque and to Aschenbach
horrible homosexual on the boat, the 'ghastly young-old man',
painted and drunken, whose simulacrum Aschenbach himself is
destined to be.

All these people belong to nightmare, as harbingers of the
world of unreason; they emerge from and merge back into the
shadowy realm of disease and pestilence, which mirrors sweet and
terrible joy. They are the landscape of the hidden world where
Aschenbach is now to become the 'solitary': the scene where this
hitherto successful and lionised public man, the master of words,
is to become an outcast, communicating only marginally with
anyone, and with his beloved, except in enigmatic glances, not at
all. 'He fled from the huddled narrow streets of the commercial
city, crossed many bridges, and came into the poor quarter of
Venice. Beggars waylaid him, the canals sickened him with their
evil exhalations' (p. 41).

Such symbols are all caught up in Venice, the most beautiful
and exotic city in the world. It is Venice that beckoned to Aschenbach from the first, as only his initial obtuseness could have
failed to see:

> He could not feel that this [his first choice for a holiday] was
> the place he sought; an inner impulse made him wretched,
> urging him on he knew not whither; he racked his brains, he
> looked up boats, then all at once his goal stood plain before
> his eyes. But of course! When one wanted to arrive overnight
> at the incomparable, the fabulous, the like-nothing-else-in-the
> world, where was it one meant? Why, obviously; he had
> intended to go there, whatever was he doing here? (p. 20)

This Venice contains Arnold's Oxford, beckoning us 'to perfection, in a word, to the ideal', and Yeats's Byzantium, where

> A starlit or a moonlit dome disdains
> All that man is,
> All mere complexities,
> The fury and the mire of human veins . . .

But, serene and apparently untouched by time, she is built on crumbling foundations and polluted waters, the child equally of religious vision and despotic greed. Where else in the plight of fallen man so visibly embodied, the divine promptings, the irrevocable commitment to sin and death? To Aschenbach, Venice is 'the fallen Queen of the seas', but she was always fallen and always Queen. Undoubtedly, this city is the fated stage for his drama, an image encompassing all other images – the pilgrim stranger, the gondoliers, the ghastly young-old man, the labyrinths of pursuit. It is the image of Tadzio – his perfect beauty united with a delicacy and a suggestion of illness; his enchanting face which is capable of 'angry disgust', 'the black and vicious language of hate' directed towards the happy, simple Russian peasants; his enigmatic responses to a lover's pursuit. Above all, it is the image of Aschenbach's own fearful fulfilment, the blazing and exotic beauty of his latter days. The streets where Aschenbach pursues and loses Tadzio are his soul, the sultry and unwholesome airs his consciousness, the depraved and corrupted inmates his destiny, the desperate refreshments his death. Death and love lock together in single images, as the plague becomes thematically inseparable (its furtive approach, its secrecy, its fatal charm and attractiveness) from the progress of love. In the end, Aschenbach is himself the plague, stalking the boy; he is the menace sensed and shunned by Tadzio's proper guardian, the fascination half-drawing the victim to itself. And it seems only one more Venetian turn – a coming out on the next jewelled church, great palace, unsuspected piazza – that Tadzio should then prove to be the angel of death. In all this, the tale is superbly Venetian, with Aschenbach hardly more than one of the daily sacrifices she might exact.

IV

Do we judge Aschenbach, or envy him? Do we pray to be delivered from, or towards, his state? It may seem tragic that so much beauty, sweetness, divinity are not allied to goodness: but what do we mean by 'goodness' in such a tale? Perhaps Aschenbach is chosen by Bacchus for punishment, as author of *The Abject*; perhaps he is chosen for particular divinity and power. If this is not essentially a tale of weakness, but of godlike sublimity, perhaps indeed Aschenbach need not be mourned?

Before we pursue this matter of appropriate moral judgements, it might be pertinent to speculate on the boy's degree of involvement with Aschenbach's love. We see this largely, of course, through the eyes of his lover, which are not the most perfect instruments for objective report. It is noteworthy that although this tale is not told in the first person, we are often directly admitted to the hero's mind. While we remain sharply enough aware that Aschenbach's situation is not to be equated with his consciousness, much of the experience is mediated directly from himself. For our sense of Tadzio, in particular, we rely very fully on what Aschenbach sees, hopes and fears. Aschenbach becomes aware (we know) of some responsiveness in Tadzio's eyes as they meet his. The youth, so courted among his peers, so guarded, spoiled and protected, has felt a novel power impinging on himself. Does he flirt mildly, and possibly without understanding; is he simply curious; or is his dawning sexuality obscurely disturbed? He may be – surely he is – Narcissus, seeking his own reflection in a distraught lover's gaze. Does he offer back fear, amusement, or the awakening power of a conqueror? Has he any adult awareness and response?

The best that Aschenbach can hope for – the violated Aschenbach of this tale – is that the boy will be sufficiently mature, and sufficiently brave, reckless or cynical, to have a brief sexual adventure on the threshold of life. The great dream is the old one of *Phaedrus* and *The Symposium*, that the sweetness of love will conquer every barrier placed in its way. Yet for a man like Aschenbach, whose whole philosophy has been a rejection of romantic extravagance and of the rejected, such a sweetly alluring idyll must be the abyss. It could only deprave and destroy his life if heeded – as indeed it does, even before he suffers the disastrous and irrevocable dream. We are forced back on the perception that he is marked out and prepared for destruction: but whether this is through his failure of will at the time of testing, or through the way of life exemplified in such a will, is not resolved.

It is in this area that the Bacchic interpretation is important; and it pervades *Death in Venice* intentionally, as we can see from the continual allusions to Euripides' play. In *The Bacchae*,

Pentheus conducts a moral crusade against Bacchus' Theban worshippers, and the god destroys him in revenge. To each god his due: this is Greek wisdom; and only a fool would behave towards the god of instinct as Pentheus does. Though his motives are honourable, they do not excuse him. He must suffer a savage personal epiphany of the god.

It is in keeping with Greek understanding that because the gods rule within man's nature as well as transcendentally, each god has a Trojan Horse in the human heart. The power of Bacchus might descend from outside as a divine possession, but it is manifested as eruption within. While this Greek insight is very far, of course, from mere psychological allegory, it includes the perception that 'repression' might precede a fall. The dark powers must be integrated into a balanced life, not pushed into exile; men must control, not deny, the forces that make them men.

Throughout Euripides' play, the Bacchic experience is proclaimed a 'joy' by the god, and by his worshippers, and prudent men take care to echo the praise. But the god openly describes his 'joy' as delusion and madness, and uses it with naked cruelty for revenge. His worshippers bless Bacchus for youth, natural energy, recovered innocence, yet they dance their dance over the abyss. There are no rational transitions as pastoral idyll yields to violence and bloodshed, only unheralded transitions, as in a dream. The whole experience exists under the species of drugged or fevered consciousness, with fitful correspondence, at best, to the world outside.

My fuller comments on these aspects must wait until later, but the truth of Euripides' vision can perhaps be agreed. Our own century is particularly well placed to acknowledge this, however greatly to its cost. We have seen the exuberant *camarderie* of Hitler's youth giving place to the concentration camps and the gas chambers, the hippie love-cult of California ending in murderous lust. Our literary culture has been particularly subject to Bacchic forces, and I shall suggest that Aschenbach's fate is prophetic of the 'soul of Europe' (with which it is explicitly linked) in our times.[1] At least from the time of *Ubu Roi* (1896) and the

---

[1] Edmund Wilson's *Axel's Castle* is now a classic study of this area of literary experience. More recent studies include Frank Kermode's *The Sense of an Ending* (Oxford U.P., New York, 1967) esp. chap. iv, and K. K. Ruthven's article 'The Savage God: Conrad and Lawrence' in the

fin de siècle, many great writers have courted the epiphany of the darker gods. As the century has progressed, so has the obsession, as any roll-call of recent culture heroes (Camus, Baldwin, Burroughs, Genet) shows. In the 1960s, it became normal to hear many traditional virtues stigmatised as 'repressive' by moralists pursuing 'freedom' in the pure Bacchic way.

A major event of the 1960s was, of course, the trial of *Lady Chatterley's Lover* as an 'obscene libel', and its vindication as a life-enhancing work. The Bacchic elements were proclaimed pure and idyllic by literary and religious experts, and new freedoms from civilisation were duly won. But there has been a coarsening of human relationships since this event, and perhaps because of it; the erotic has increasingly been exalted as an end. Loyalty, tenderness, honour have faded from sexual consciousness, to be replaced by orgasms, abortions, full frontal nudity and pills. In the 1960s, many young people pursued the Bacchic fulfilments in a pop and drugs 'culture', and found the realities of squalor, brutality and death.

One significant aspect is that most of the major writers of the early twentieth century are not themselves responsible (though Lawrence cannot escape without blame). Many of them depicted the actually dark side of the dark gods memorably and beautifully, as Mann does in the work before us now. The paradox, rather, is that while such early moderns treated the instinctual powers with fitting fear as well as reverence, their critics have usually followed a simpler way. The sombre insights of Yeats and Eliot, even, have been denounced as 'fascist', by critics led by messianic and utopian lights. Primitivism has flourished indeed in the surely alien soil of modern history, to a degree which only Bacchic hallucination seems to explain. The dark powers have been hailed as joy and salvation, pure and simple, in defiance of all human experience present and past.

Pentheus' punishment in Euripides' play (to return to this) is made inevitable by the fact that a man cannot really exile the more dangerous parts of his nature, or successfully cauterise his inner self. To reject Bacchus is as dangerous as accepting him too totally, since the god must and will have his dues. Pentheus eventually agrees (like Aschenbach) to go 'half-way to the tigers', and

tenth anniversary issue of the *Critical Quarterly* (C. B. Cox and A. E. Dyson (eds.), *Word in the Desert*, Oxford U.P., 1968).

his hidden instincts leap within their cage. The god first lures him into the fatal breakdown of vigilance, and then addresses insidious suggestions to the traitor within. Deceived by the promise of invisibility (a direct lie, like much else that Bacchus tells him), Pentheus parades through the streets dressed as a woman, and is delivered over to dismemberment and death. His suppressed voyeurism and transvestism are the god's weapons, and no mercy is finally shown. In *Death in Venice*, Aschenbach's terrible dream is the parallel incident, and what he dreams *is* the climax of Euripides' play.

Like Pentheus, in fact, Aschenbach must be wrested from his hard-won dignity and propriety, and consigned to the destructive powers he has tried to resist. As the reckless obsession with Tadzio gathers, he must not be spared the delusion of recovered youth and bliss. This must be played off also against those occasional horrifyingly different glimpses of his predicament, thrown up by the suppressed but not extinguished rational powers. There comes the moment when he allows a barber to transform him into the semblance of the 'ghastly young-old man' of the Venice quayside, and throws his concern for respect and survival to the winds. He must suffer this violation of all he has chosen, revered and shaped himself towards, for the joy which seems to transcend a lifetime of work.

Like Pentheus he must wonder whether he recovers sanity in Venice, or whether he is plunged into madness and total shame. Does he belong with Antony and Tristram, Lancelot and Troilus, among the great doomed lovers; or is he any elderly man led to forfeit repute, and the ideals he has lived for, by one forbidden, fierce and seemingly irresistible joy? While any reader who judges too easily will be brutally insensitive, the most brutal condemnations are endorsed in his heart.

In worldly terms, we are challenged to attempt judgements and left to move through the novel's data as we can. The colouring I have pointed to is chiefly Hellenic, but other modes of understanding are also invoked. There is the intellectual analysis which is persistently obtruded, for instance, of Aschenbach as a man irrevocably split into warring halves. These are associated with his 'bourgeois' father and his 'bohemian' mother, who are seen as contributing irreconcilable traits to the mix. In my view, this aspect of the novel is naïve, and its one structural weakness, but it usefully links us back to *Tonio Kröger* (1903). It is also of a piece with Aschenbach's role as a typical modern hero, on which my main conclusions will turn.

V

The young Aschenbach finds himself torn between 'bourgeois' and 'artist', and could echo the words of Tonio Kröger: 'I stand between two worlds. I am at home in neither, and I suffer in consequence.' But even in youth he has shunned indolence, and the vices which Tonio Kröger resorts to, in favour of discipline and will. The desire for fame, which preserves him from despair and dissipation, becomes the guiding passion of his life. Unlike Tonio Kröger, he does not allow 'obscure impulse' to rule him, but learns to reunite impulse with direction and power.

In middle life Aschenbach becomes famous as author of *The Abject*, 'which taught a whole grateful generation that a man can still be capable of moral resolution even after he has plumbed the depths of self-knowledge'. This salvation involves, however, a rejection of all those who fall in life's battle, and a resolute flight from their bitterness and from their claims. 'With rage the author here rejects the rejected, casts out the outcast' . . . 'explicitly he renounces sympathy with the abyss'. Aschenbach pushes the very pains of art into bourgeois service, making art itself a text for disciplined hard work.

In escaping the abyss, then, Aschenbach sacrifices certain freedoms of love and sympathy, including perhaps the inner freedom of his art. This lends an obvious ironic fitness to his nemesis in *Death in Venice*, though it could also, of course, be read another way. A stern moralist might decide that Aschenbach dies shamefully because he relapses from chastened insight, and proves unable to evade his private abyss. Was it not St Paul who said, 'I keep under my body and bring it unto subjection: lest that by any means, when I have preached to others, I myself should be a castaway'?

Yet to read *Death in Venice* as an artist's warning against himself is surely too literal, if only because it ignores the existence and force of the work itself. Mann is not Aschenbach, nor is *Death in Venice* the story of *Death in Venice*; there is also the usual miracle of form. If Aschenbach's adventure is in fact surrounded with richness and transmuted to beauty, the form which achieves this cannot be merely a lie. Few readers are likely to judge Aschenbach without fear and pity, or to imagine that they might themselves be exempt from his fate. The moral sensitivity generated is clearly higher than self-righteousness, and more human than any mere armour-plating against suffering and love. As we come to understand the extent to which Aschenbach's 'bourgeois' days were themselves armour-plated, we sense that he dies a finer, though a less reputable, man than he lived.

To point this out is, of course, to risk stating the obvious; but it is also to suggest a coarseness in Mann's intellectual structure when compared with his art. The antithesis between 'bourgeois' and 'bohemian' is bound to seem blunt and unsatisfactory when embedded in so subtle and beautiful a tale. It offers little to our real understanding of Aschenbach's predicament, and is at odds with the novel's manifest power. Whatever we make of Aschenbach's encounter with the god he has made a stranger, we are unlikely to extract simple insights about class, or about art.

That Aschenbach's sufferings turn to beauty in the telling is, as I have insisted, a triumph of form. Whatever doubts about form *Death in Venice* expresses, the tale itself is free to whisper and sing. It is one of those works of art which enriches our education, humanises our culture, haunts our imaginations, safeguards our religion itself. In forcing us to take account of the sublime and tragic, it forces us back with its hero, towards the abyss.

Since this triumph is achieved by content and form in indissoluble unity, we can be sure that Apollo as well as Dionysus has his dues. There is a reminder that morality in a work of art is never autonomous, and can never therefore be abstracted on its own. Because the content is inseparable from texture, structure, tone, symbolism and language, there can be no ultimate divide between meaning and form. And since the artist's sensitivity is inevitably incarnate in his creation, refined sensitivity is seen to be one of the conditions of greatness in art.

While such reflections may not answer all the doubts about art which afflict Aschenbach, they direct us away from the cramping framework in which he thinks. Art clearly cannot be simply 'bourgeois' in the sense indicated, but neither can it be simply anarchic in 'bohemian' ways. The tale transcends its intellectual framework by its own achievement; and in doing this, it offers us a useful further clue. Is it possible that other morals can be drawn by a reader of *Death in Venice*, perhaps in defiance, almost, of its chosen terms?

VI

With this in mind, I now want to look at Aschenbach's sufferings from a different perspective, and to consider the novel's intellectual framework alongside the novel itself. Aschenbach is specifically linked in Mann's opening pages with the 'soul of Europe', and while his personal fate is unique, and remote from normal experience, we are also invited to see him as 'typical' in certain ways. The 'soul of Europe' is a concept familiar in Arnold, Eliot and many other great writers, and gives a positive nudge in the direction of cultural debate.

My suggestion will be that Aschenbach's whole development as we see it is post-Christian, and that this is even truer of his middle years as author of *The Abject*, than it is of his youthful cynicism, or his last great love. It may indeed be that his experience links so fruitfully with the ethos of Plato and Euripides precisely because he is a distinctively *modern* man. Ancient and modern meet, in certain tragic insights and torments, partly because the great intervening episode of Christian Europe has come and gone. It it is almost as though St Paul had never stood before the altar of the Unknown God in Athens, and spoken his marvellous and astonishing words.

In saying this, I am not implying that Christianity during its ascendancy directly influenced everyone, nor that it influences no one today. And I am not implying personal moral judgements against Aschenbach, or arguing that no Christian hero could have met with his fate. What I have in mind rather is that range of human possibilities – ways of thought, common assumptions and directions – which were generally operative in Christian Europe even upon minds not committed to them, and which are no longer part of our cultural life. They have ceased to influence either the minds which direct our culture or the lives of most people, and exist only for those – *if* for those – who 'believe'. Our loss has resulted, I believe, in a brutalisation of society and an impoverishment of humanity, to which *Death in Venice* supplies some important clues.

I assume that in any Christian context other than a wholly insensitive or perverted one, Aschenbach's life and thought could not have developed as they do. Just as he would have been less tormented by the desire to justify art as an end in itself in his early days, so he would never have sought the 'bourgeois' way out. Even if certain late Victorian capitalists might have confused their religion with middle-class morality, no sensitive believer could have made the mistake. The whole contrast between a 'respectable' world safe from the abyss and an abysmal world given over to chaos and anarchy belongs to a time when Christian thinking had ceased generally to count. The Christian God descends into the abyss to save the rejected by being rejected, and is as far removed from *The Abject* as from the devil himself. In this aspect, Aschenbach foreshadows a more modern ethos, which offers cultural alternatives – often stark ones – attuned to a secular age.

We next notice that the alternatives which polarise Aschenbach's thinking, and on which I have commented earlier, are familiar in even cruder forms today. Most of our cultural thinking tends towards oversimplifications, of a kind strikingly similar to his. We are constantly confronted with analyses conducted in quasi-Marxist or quasi-Freudian terminology, which suggest no viable alternatives between dire extremes. These usually turn on the notion that social or moral authority is 'repressive', 'fascist' or otherwise destructive, and that 'freedom' demands the total autonomy of 'self'. In between such alternatives those who talk sense are nearly always located, but the alternatives insistently press themselves to the fore. More importantly, the tug-of-war over vital public structures and institutions is conducted in terms of the opposites, with schools, universities, churches, authorities of all kinds and at all levels, torn, often quite literally, between the two. It is little to the point that few of the institutions resemble such alternatives in practice, if the forces which make or unmake them run to extremes. This degree of oversimplification, now highly characteristic of a secular society, seems foreshadowed in the severely antithetical ideas and commitments of Aschenbach. Who but heretics, in the Christian centuries, would have seen a total split – and of this kind – between 'bohemian' and 'bourgeois', or suspected that love and discipline are at opposite poles?

But if Aschenbach's 'respectable' life is obviously, in a sensitive man, post-Christian, so is the form which his love for Tadzio takes. And here again, I must try to guard against two possible misunderstandings, either of which would misrepresent what I mean. That *Death in Venice* is subtle and beautiful, I have already attested; and I do not doubt its psychological truth. The progress of Aschenbach's love is charted with exquisite fidelity, through every tone and nuance of the tale. At the same time, I am not arguing – most certainly not – that a Christian hero would be immune to Bacchus, or that he could not behave and die, as a sinner, in a similar way. There are many tormented lovers in Christian fiction, and the literature of this does not lie. And I am not suggesting – to be totally explicit – that Aschenbach is less moral or less sensitive because he is post-Christian, or that this matter at all affects our moral response, as readers, to his fate. What I am saying is that a Christian hero would move in a sharply different intellectual and spiritual ambiance, and would not seem typical of the modern 'soul of Europe' in at all this way. He might fall disastrously in love and be destroyed in the outcome, but he would not fall disastrously in love like this. The mental and spiritual colourings would be different, with a range of guilt, hope, fear, prayer and aspiration wholly distinct from anything we see. Whether these different colourings would save a Christian hero is another matter, and they would relate to a different – and hypothetical – tale. But they would present him with richer and fuller human possibilities of loving, and make the idea of love a much less shameful affair. He would suffer – if he did suffer – in a finer and subtler atmosphere than Aschenbach, even if he were less fine and subtle himself. He would not (to return to this) start from a Tonio Krögerish cynicism, move on to write *The Abject*, and end totally collapsed in a rejected abyss. It is doubtful whether his end would surprise him as much as it surprises Aschenbach, or seem so totally at variance with his professions and his ideals. He would die as a sinner, and hope for grace.

As a way of pursuing what I have in mind, I want to return to the nature of Aschenbach's obsession. In one obvious way his love for Tadzio marks him out as a man better than average but less than perfect (an Aristotelian tragic hero, in fact). A perfect person would be as safe from Bacchus as Milton's Lady is from Comus; but such perfection is admittedly rare. A depraved per-

son would also be safe, or at least much safer, since he would
hardly obsess himself with erotic impossibilities or be caught by the
erotic unawares. Aschenbach's experience is that of a man who is
sensitive to beauty, tender and considerate by nature, but also
insulated from very much knowledge of his sexual depths.

But, this might suggest, is he not thereby a victim of sexual
ignorance, and to this extent a pre-Freudian rather than a post-
Christian man? And it may be true that those of us brought up on
Freud would be less likely than Aschenbach to overlook a homosexual component, or to imagine that growing love could be totally
insulated from sex. But this is not to my mind the important
aspect of *Death in Venice*, and indeed it seems hardly important
at all. What really counts is Aschenbach's reaction to self-
knowledge when it comes to him: as soon as he recognises the
erotic he submits to it and ceases to experience love apart from
his need. It is here that we encounter the particularly and distinctively modern attitude which marks the 'soul of Europe' in our
times. One could say that, while post-Freudians are less likely to
overlook sexual possibilities in their love than most of their pre-
decessors, they are far more likely to overlook almost everything
else. They are more likely to overlook love itself, in its Christian
aspect, as Aschenbach clearly and disastrously does. In Christian
terms, it would be perfectly possible for him to say of the boy –
either in his heart, or aloud – 'I love you', and for this to be no
matter for concealment or incipient shame. St John represents
himself as 'the disciple whom Jesus loved', who leaned on Jesus's
breast at the last supper, and 'love' has always been triumphant in
the Church. In essence, it is delighted homage to a loved person,
a salute from 'self' to the glories outside. The profession of love
is natural to St John, and immensely rewarding, even in a
relationship where sex could not possibly come. It is surely post-
Christian for the words 'I love you' to seem inherently dangerous,
as the prelude – where sex is impossible – to suffering and shame.

Now it might be argued that Aschenbach's love is in fact erotic,
or becomes so, and that such reflections are therefore beside the
point. But I think that his love becomes erotic and obsessive
partly, at least, because this is all it can be. When recognised as
love, eroticism becomes the sole possibility, with friendship a non-
starter in the race. Aschenbach's love becomes his desire to possess
Tadzio, and this supersedes his reverence for the boy's beauty and

graces – for the boy himself. The betraying fact is not the erotic desire which might happen to anyone, but the egocentric possessiveness also aroused. In the Christian ethos, it would have seemed natural to love widely and passionately across all barriers of age, sex, race and colour, but not natural to regard possessive and erotic demands as a *sine qua non*. On the contrary, such demands would be seen as totally harmful except in marriage, and the surest way of soiling and destroying love. What has disappeared, with this Christian perspective, is the sense that, since love is drawn out in homage to another person, it links only contingently, if at all, with the lover's needs.

It seems probable that Aschenbach's rejection of the rejected directly relates, as a post-Christian phenomenon, to the disastrous turn which his love later takes. The kind of self-discipline which mistrusts love and raises barriers against it may be precisely the kind which responds, as Aschenbach's does, to irresistible love. If the rejection of the rejected is one distinctively post-Christian doctrine, so still more is the related fear of love. Aschenbach lays himself open to nemesis then not only in the terms recognised by the Greeks and by modern psychologists, but in terms central – however neglected they have often been – to the Christian Church.

VII

My suggestion, it will be seen, is that friendship – a love rich and pervasive in Christian life and literature – has been the chief casualty of our modern obsession with sex. That our sexual instincts are better understood today, is of course reassuring, as indeed is our greater tolerance towards deviant sex. But such gains have been won at great cost in confusion and suffering, which Aschenbach's story illustrates especially well. The losses stem from a strange and illogical leap from the understanding that deep love usually arouses sexual feelings, to the dogma that sex is love's root cause and sole end. The next step is the assumption that sexual feelings cannot be vetoed by grace and willpower where they are inappropriate, but that they must be inflamed, rather, until they goad and destroy. This confusion goes back beyond Freud to the early Romantics, and has its distant primitivist precursors in the ancient world. It turns on a view of human relationships which has been a minority report in most periods, but has become overwhelmingly the majority report in the past twenty years. This is the notion that the 'self' is the sole source of its own laws and the sole arbiter – its own judge, its own appeal court, its own god. From here, it has followed that relationships have become a matter of need, not of homage, and increasingly – here modern psychology has certainly been influential – of biological need. The 'self', rejecting all external bearings, including good sense and decency, has harvested sexual sufferings on the grandest scale.

A major victim has been the Christian perception that while sex cannot exist in its highest forms without love and affection, love and affection are always distinct from, and higher than, sex. For Donne in 'The Extasie' (to take one of many possible instances), sex is the physical incarnation of spiritual love. Sex might become the physical sign of love and its bodily consummation, but the origin of love is greater and invisible, in the soul. Donne also proceeded of course to sexual excesses which he recognised as sinful, but he nowhere confused sex with love. In the Christian centuries it was also known that the self must deny itself to live, die to be fruitful, and that rebirth is as vital to love as to salvation itself. What greater definition of love is there than this one from the New Testament, which points so totally and completely away from the self? 'Greater love hath no man than this, that a man lay down his life for his friends.' The freedoms of such love, which meet us time and again in previous centuries, can be looked for in modern literature almost in vain.[1]

Turning back to *Death in Venice*, I am struck most of all by the absences. Why does Aschenbach never envisage fruitful love between himself and Tadzio, or any healing or beneficial outcome of his love? He could have introduced himself to the family with propriety and sought appropriate expressions of love. Mann makes clear indeed that he precipitates his fate by failing to speak to the family – to warn them of plague, cultivate them, put himself on a friendly footing – and that this isolation is the soil where his sufferings grow.

In this conclusion I am ranging beyond Mann's intellectual context, but in a way which I believe he leaves his readers free to

[1] For a particularly fine instance, see the quotation from Milton's *An Apology for Smectymnuus*, p. 17 above.

do. To my mind the tragic essence is to be located in the cultural disaster of our times. While Christianity has been continually attacked by enemies for its supposed laws and restrictions against love, the same enemies have created the conditions they deplore. Inside Christianity, love has always been released widely and freely, with joy and without torment, inside the simple, if difficult, law of dying to self. We have had, to take the most striking instance, the words of the marriage vow, which seem the very linguistic structure of love. We have had the tradition of deep and enduring friendship, which Christian literature has so often celebrated. It has remained for a romantic culture to mistake these conditions of freedom for arbitrary restrictions, and to imagine that unfettered instinct is a truer arbiter of love. In place of Christian freedom, we have an ethos which has surrounded love with squalor and embarrassment, and pushed it towards obsessiveness and fear. The nag of lust has been turned first into social virtue, and then into the beginning, middle and end of personal relationships. Our most distinctive moral crusades are now for nudity, pornography, obscenity, and, of course, for the inalienable right of children to be depraved. The resulting society is mirrored in Genet, Nabokov, Burroughs, Mailer, Baldwin, *Oh! Calcutta*, *Hair* – most of our novels, most of our plays and films; where does such a list stop? It is in these places that future generations will find us, and judge what degree of freedom in love we really have.

My suggestion is not that Aschenbach at all shares in so much modern squalor, but that he is a symptom of the forces which shaped it half a century ago. As recently as 1850, Dickens could depict David Copperfield's love for Steerforth, Tennyson could write and publish *In Memoriam*; the traditional Christian channels still flowed. If such relationships are less often expressed and perhaps less often purely experienced in the 1970s, then the absences from *Death in Venice* could be one of our clues. And of course it is not only loves like Aschenbach's which are now pertinent: the mass has spread to 'normal' sexuality, including – often – marriage itself.

The 'stranger god' Mann refers us to is, we know, Bacchus; but in *Death in Venice* there is another, and far greater, stranger God.

6 Faith Among the Ashes: Scott Fitzgerald's *The Great Gatsby*

> Gatsby must have looked up at an unfamiliar sky
> through frightening leaves and shivered as he found
> what a grotesque thing a rose is and how raw the
> sunlight was upon the scarcely created grass. A new
> world, material without being real, where poor ghosts,
> breathing dreams like air, drifted fortuitously about. . . .

I

In 1925 T. S. Eliot found himself as moved and interested by *The Great Gatsby* as he had been by any novel for a very long time. Since then, the novel has attracted praise from a great many discriminating critics on both sides of the Atlantic, and the deep interest of first-generation readers has been shared by others coming from different backgrounds and at a later time. Any new consideration must now be concerned with it then as a work which belongs not only to American but to world literature; not only to the immediate soil from which it sprang (prohibition, big business, gangsters, jazz, uprootedness) but to the tragic record of men 'without God, and without hope in the world'. This is worth stating, if only because an English critic might otherwise feel diffident about approaching a masterpiece which in many ways is so distinctively American, and which has been cited so often in histories of the American dream. An Englishman will miss, no doubt, some important nuances that to an American will be immediately obvious. He will be less sure of himself than an American critic might be in assessing how far Fitzgerald does, or does not, look forward to Salinger, Bellow and other writers of the affluent, or the alienated, society. He might hope, however, to see other things (and I am relieved to find Leo Marx lending support to this) which will prove no less important in a total reading and assessment, and which might be less easily perceptible at home than abroad. This at any rate must be my excuse for venturing to by-pass the type of sociological interest usually and rightly displayed, and to consider *Gatsby* as something even bigger than the demythologising, or remythologising, of the American soul. The squalor and splendour of Gatsby's dreams belong – like Aschenbach's – to humanity, as does the irony, and judgement, of his awakening.

II

The action takes place in 'the waste land' (this phrase is used), and is, at one level, the study of a broken society. The 'valley of ashes' in which Myrtle and Wilson live symbolises the human situation in an age of chaos. It is 'a certain desolate area of land' in which 'ash grey men' swarm dimly, stirring up 'an impenetrable cloud, which screens their obscure operations from your sight.' This devitalised limbo is presided over by the eyes of Dr T. J. Eckleburg.

> The eyes of Dr T. J. Eckleburg are blue and gigantic – their retinas are one yard high. They look out of no face, but instead, from a pair of enormous yellow spectacles which pass over a non-existent nose.

Dr Eckleburg is an advertisement for spectacles, now faded and irrelevant: put there by some 'wild wag of an oculist' who has himself, by this time, either sunk down 'into eternal blindness, or forgot them and moved away'. As a simple but haunting symbol of the *deus absconditus* who might once have set the waste land in motion, Dr Eckleburg recurs at certain crucial moments in the novel. He is the only religious reference, but his sightless gaze precludes the possibility of judging the 'ash grey men' against traditional religious norms, and confers upon them the right to pity as well as to scorn. It ensures too that, though the actual setting of the valley is American, and urban, and working-class (I intend to use the word 'class' throughout this account, without apology), the predicament, as in Eliot's own *Waste Land*, is universal.

Beneath Dr Eckleburg's unseeing eyes the ash-grey men drift. 'Drift' is a word used many times in the novel, not only of Gatsby himself, who alone among the characters thinks he knows where he is going, but also of Daisy, Tom and all the main characters, including Carraway the narrator.

Tom and Daisy, the 'moneyed' class, have for years 'drifted

here and there unrestfully wherever people played polo and were rich together'. Tom's restlessness is an arrogant assertiveness seeking to evade in bluster the deep uneasiness of self-knowledge. His hypocrisy and lack of human feeling make him the most unpleasant character in the book, but he is also, when it comes to the point, one of the sanest. In the battle with Gatsby he has the nature of things on his side, so that his victory is as inevitable as it is unadmirable. The discovery that his sanity is even less worth while in human terms than Gatsby's self-centred fantasy is not the least of the novel's ironies.

Daisy is more complex than Tom, and far less real. Her manner has in it, as Carraway notes, all the promise of the world. Her eyes, 'looking up into my face, promised that there was no one in the world she so much wanted to see'; her voice held 'a promise that she had done gay, exciting things just a while since, and that there were gay, exciting things hovering in the same hour'. But this is all yesterday and tomorrow. Today, there is only emptiness. 'What'll we do with ourselves this afternoon?' cried Daisy, 'and the day after that, and the next thirty years?'

When Gatsby arrives with his 'romantic readiness', his unqualified faith in Daisy's ideal and absolute reality, he is broken against her sheer non-existence. She turns out to be literally nothing, and vanishes from the novel at the very point when, if she existed at all, she would have to start being really there. Her romantic façade, so adequate in appearance to the dreams Gatsby has built around it, is without reality. She has no belief in it herself, and so it means nothing. It is no more than an attempt to alchemise the dreariness of an unsuccessful life into some esoteric privilege of the sophisticated. The account she gives of her 'cynicism' is not without genuine pain. But the pain is transmuted in the telling into a pleasure – the only genuine pleasure, one feels, of which she is capable.

> The moment her voice broke off, ceasing to compel my attention, my belief, I felt the basic insincerity of what she had said. . . . I waited, and sure enough, in a moment she looked at me with an absolute smirk on her lovely face, as if she had asserted her membership in a rather distinguished secret society to which she and Tom belonged.

Behind the façade of the rich, the 'rather distinguished secret society' to which they belong, is money and carelessness – the two protections upon which they fall back in moments of crisis, leaving those outside to sink or swim.

The social break-up at this level is paralleled in the working class. Myrtle, Tom's mistress, is the quintessence of vulgarity. Her 'class' is no strong, peasant culture, but a drifting wreckage of the spiritless and defeated. Her only hope is to escape – and it is her one positive quality, her vitality, which leads her to seek happiness in a role other than that to which she is born. With Tom's prestige and money behind her she sets up a town establishment, throws parties, apes the rich, outgrows her husband ('I thought he knew something about breeding, but he wasn't fit to lick my shoe'), looks down on her own class with aloof disdain. ('Myrtle raised her eyebrows at the shiftlessness of the lower orders. "Those people! You have to keep after them all the time".') In playing this moneyed role, she achieves most of its actual corruptions whilst adding the new ingredient of vulgarity. One minute she avoids the word 'bitch' when buying a dog ('Is it a boy or a girl?' she asked delicately), the next takes for granted that a total stranger will want to sleep with her sister.

And yet, in a universe of ash-grey men represented by her husband and presided over by the eyes of Dr Eckleburg, it is difficult to feel she is very obviously to blame. Fitzgerald's ironic awareness of life's perversities is symbolised in the fact that her one positive quality, her vitality, should find expression in the waste land only as vulgarity and disloyalty, and that it should become the instrument of her death. In the same way, Gatsby's great positive quality – his faith, and the loyalty to Daisy that goes with it – finds expression only as a tawdry self-centredness, and it too contributes to his death.

III

Among these rootless people Carraway comes to live, and to be in some degree involved in their lives. This implication is impersonal, in that his own emotions and destiny are not centrally at issue, personal in that his humanity forces him, though against his will, to respond. The tone of the narrative is his to control; and as he comes to understand and pity Gatsby, the novel moves from comedy to a tragic key. Carraway's involvement amounts in the end to a useless but not uncostly selflessness, which turns out to be the most important moral positive the novel has to offer.

Carraway is the one middle-class character in the novel – vaguely at home in the worlds both of Daisy and of Myrtle, but belonging to neither, and so able to see and judge both very clearly. He is conscious of 'advantages' of moral education that enable him to see through false romanticisms to their underlying insincerity, and savour their bitter ironies. Yet he too has his restlessness, as uprooted as everyone else in truth, though more determined than the rest to preserve some 'decencies', to cling to some principle of order and sanity in the wreckage.

His family comes from the Middle West. It is proud of having a Duke somewhere in the family tree, but relies in practice for its safety and self-respect on big business – the 'wholesale hardware business' which Carraway never wholly loses sight of as his birthright. He has been made restless by the war, and is now looking for some sort of armour against life in detachment and moral alertness. The 'intimate revelations of young men' bore him. He is tolerant of other people, but would escape from the sloughs of emotional despond into some simple pattern of control and acceptance.

> Conduct may be founded on the hard rock or the wet marshes, but after a certain point I don't care what it is founded on. When I came back from the East last autumn I felt that I wanted the world to be in uniform and at a sort of moral attention for ever; I wanted no more riotous excursions, with privileged glimpses into the human heart.

Cast into the situation which is the subject of the novel, his attitude is from the first ambivalent. 'I was within and without, simultaneously enchanted and repelled by the inexhaustible variety of life.' He sees the sordidness, the unreality of the New York 'rich', and his ironic observation upon them is habitually devastating. But he is able to hope, even while seeing as clearly as he does, that the vitality, the variety, the promise of excitement, may not be wholly false. Infected with the restlessness that he records in others, he is half convinced that some rewarding experience might lie behind the world of throbbing taxis, rich perfumes, gay parties, if one could only find the magic key. 'I began to like New York, the racy, adventurous feel of it at night, and the satisfaction that the constant flicker of men and women and machines gives to the restless eye.' He responds almost equally to the haunting loneliness of it, and the unceasing promise. His imagination is willing to entertain what his intellect and experience of life rejects: 'Imagining that I, too, was hurrying towards gaiety and sharing their intimate excitement, I wished them well.'

Caraway's attitude towards Gatsby is, from the first, typical. He recognises in Gatsby the epitome of his society, and is accordingly enchanted and repelled by him in the highest degree. His conscious moral instinct is to disapprove; but his imagination is fascinated since perhaps here, in this extraordinary man, the romantic promise is at last fulfilled. He wavers therefore between almost complete contempt for Gatsby and almost complete faith in him; and this ambivalent attitude persists until Gatsby's collapse, after which it gives way to a deeper, and costlier, attitude of pity towards which the whole novel moves. The eventual shattering of Gatsby's high romantic hopes against an inexorably unromantic reality turns him, for Carraway, into a tragic figure. The quality of the ironic observation reflects this change, and Carraway's closing meditation, rising above the particular events, finds a universal and tragic significance in Gatsby's fate.

IV

Carraway's first mention of the hero, some time before he actually appears, is a clear statement of his own judgement upon him: 'Gatsby, who represented everything for which I have an unaffected scorn.' But it is an acknowledgement also of the fascination which Gatsby exerts over him. 'If personality is an unbroken series of successful gestures, then there was something gorgeous about him, some heightened sensitivity to the promise of life.'

In one sense Gatsby is the apotheosis of his rootless society. His background is cosmopolitan, his past a mystery, his temperament that of an opportunist entirely oblivious to the claims of people or the world outside. His threadbare self-dramatisation, unremitting selfishness, and attempts to make something out of nothing are the same in kind as those of the waste-land society, and different only in intensity. Yet this intensity springs from a quality which he alone has: and this we might call 'faith'. He really believes in himself and his illusions; and this quality of faith, however grotesque it must seem with such an object, sets his apart from the cynically armoured midgets whom he epitomises. It makes him bigger than they are, and more vulnerable. It is also a quality which commands respect from Carraway: since at the very least, 'faith' protects Gatsby from the evasiveness, the conscious hypocrisy of the Toms and Daisies of the world, conferring something of the heroic on what he does; and at the best it might still turn out to be the 'way in' to some kind of reality beyond the romantic façade, the romantic alchemy which, despite his cynicism, Carraway still half hopes one day to find.

Gatsby's first appearance is in his garden at night looking out at the single green light which is the symbol of his dreams. He is content to 'be alone'; and isolation is an essential part of his make-up, a necessary part of his god-like self-sufficiency. He is next heard of as a mystery, the man whom nobody knows, but whose hospitality everybody accepts.

> There was music from my neighbour's house through the summer night. In his blue gardens men and girls came and went like moths among the whisperings and the champagne and the stars.

When Carraway meets him as a host, and first hears that 'old sport' which becomes so moving at the end, he does not even know that it *is* Gatsby. This social gaffe is an occasion for the sublime courtesy and forgiveness that Gatsby has to dispense, the 'charm' which is too deeply a part of his act for any accusation of insincerity to be even remotely appropriate.

> He smiled understandingly – much more than understandingly. It was one of those rare smiles with a quality of eternal reassurance in it, that you may come across four or five times in life. It faced – or seemed to face – the whole eternal world for an instant, and then concentrated on *you* with an irresistible prejudice in your favour. It understood you just so far as you wanted to be understood, believed in you as you would like to believe in yourself, and assured you that it had precisely the impression of you that, at your best, you hoped to convey. Precisely at that point it vanished. . . .

As Gatsby's guests become more hilarious, his own 'correctness' grows. He is apart from the chaos which his money has mysteriously called into being, presiding over it with benevolent detachment: considerate to his fellows when they are careless, decorous when they are disorderly. As the party finishes, he remains alone on the steps of his mansion – his formality and his solitude an intriguing enigma, that has still to be explored.

A sudden emptiness seemed to flow now from the windows and the doors, endowing with complete isolation the figure of the host, who stood on the porch, his hand up in a formal gesture of farewell.

V

This then is the setting. The novel is concerned with Gatsby's reasons for appearing out of the blue and becoming host to half the rich 'moths' of New York. He is, it turns out, in love with Daisy. The whole elaborate decor has been constructed for the sole purpose of staging a dramatic reunion with her: a reunion which will impress her with Gatsby's 'greatness', and eradicate, at a stroke, the five years of married life which she has drifted through since seeing him last.

As we soon learn, his affair with Daisy had been a youthful romance, one among many, and nurtured in an atmosphere of cynicism, purposelessness and deceit. But unlike Gatsby's other affairs it had been complicated first by Daisy's casualness, and then by their unavoidable separation; and somehow, during the muddle, Gatsby had fallen in love, and the affair had become the 'greatest thing in his life'. The romantic promise which in Daisy herself was the merest façade became, for him, an ideal, an absolute reality. He built around her the dreams and fervours of his youth: adolescent, self-centred, fantastic, yet also untroubled by doubt and therefore strong; attracting to themselves the best as well as the worst of his qualities, and eventually becoming an obsession of the most intractable kind.

As Carraway comes to know Gatsby, he wavers between scepticism and faith. He sees clearly in Gatsby the faults which he scorns in others – 'charm' that is simply a technique for success, self-centredness masquerading as heroic vision, romantic pretensions based on economic corruption and a total disregard for humanity – yet he is impressed, despite himself, by the faith which transmutes all this into another pattern. Gatsby is different from the others in that he means every word he says, and really believes in his uniqueness. His romantic clichés, unlike those of Tom or Daisy, are used with simple belief that they are his own discovery, his own prerogative, his own guarantee of Olympian apartness and election. He is 'trying to forget something very sad that happened . . . long ago'. He has 'tried very hard to die but seemed to bear an enchanted life'. To listen to him is like 'skimming hastily through a dozen mazagines' – and yet is not like that at all, since Gatsby's faith really has brought the dead clichés back to life, or some semblance of life. So much in his account that might have been empty boasting turns out to be true. He really has been to Oxford – after a fashion. His credentials from the commissioner of police for whom he was 'able to do . . . a favour once' are genuine enough to prevent him from being arrested for breaking a traffic law. His love for Daisy is also real, up to a point: there is a moment when it seems that he has achieved the impossible, and actually realised his fantastic programme for returning to the past.

The tragedy – for it is a tragic novel, though of an unorthodox kind – lies in the fact that Gatsby can go only so far and no further. Faith can still remove sizeable molehills, but is absolutely powerless when it comes to mountains. The ultimate romantic affirmation, 'I'll always love you alone', cannot be brought to life: certainly not in the waste land; not when people like Daisy and Gatsby himself, are involved. Gatsby's faith has to break, in the end, against a reality radically incompatible with it. But in so breaking, it makes him a tragic figure, uniting him symbolically with many more worthy than himself – with, indeed, the general tragic lot of mankind.

VI

Gatsby's whole project is characterised by that mingling of the fantastic and the scrupulously correct which is his settled attitude to life (the phrase 'old sport' is itself a masterly fusion of the two extremes). He approaches Carraway with his all-important request not directly, but by way of Jordan Baker. And why? Because 'Miss Baker's a great sportswoman, you know, and she'd never do anything that wasn't right'. His 'correctness' like most of his other qualities is peculiarly inverted, but not wholly a sham. He uses it exclusively to get his own way, and yet he is so wholly taken-in himself that he cannot be accused, as anyone else might be, of hypocrisy.

And what *does* Gatsby want of Carraway? 'He wants to know,' continued Jordan, 'if you'll invite Daisy to your house some afternoon and then let him come over.'

He wants Carraway, to put this bluntly, to help him capture a friend's wife – and this simply because Carraway happens to be the man living next door, from which a spectacular view of the Gatsby mansion is to be enjoyed. 'The modesty of the demand shook me,' Carraway comments; and it is part of the greatness of the novel that, though Carraway sees the whole situation very clearly, and has no bias in favour either of emotional extravagance or of Gatsby himself, his comment is not wholly ironical. It is not even primarily ironical, since Carraway is already beginning to see also, in all its tawdry splendour, the nature of Gatsby's vision; and given that, the demand really is modest.

> He had waited five years and bought a mansion where he dispensed starlight to casual moths – so that he could 'come over' some afternoon to a stranger's garden.

Carraway's comment to Jordan ('Did I have to know all this before he could ask such a little thing?') is again only marginally ironic. The situation is too unanchored for simple moral judgements – partly because, given Gatsby's faith among the ashes, it is difficult to find norms against which to judge; partly because Gatsby is, after all, 'big', so that nothing he does can be simply contemptible; and partly because Carraway himself is not given to conventional attitudes towards human relations, so that his judgement rises out of a growing awareness of a complex situation and is in no sense imported from outside. He readily agrees in any event to Gatsby's request, his 'unaffected scorn' of the man wholly overcome now by fascinated interest in the unfolding events.

The actual meeting of Gatsby and Daisy is the central episode of the novel. Everything leads up to it, and what follows is a working out of implications which are in the meeting itself. There is the tension as Gatsby waits, and the embarrassing absurdity of the first few minutes together – the irony here highly comic, and very much at Gatsby's expense. Then comes the moment of happiness, when the ideal seems to have been actualised. Daisy herself is carried away by the elation of the moment. ' "I'm glad Jay." Her throat, full of . . . aching, grieving beauty, told only of her unexpected joy.' And Gatsby is transfigured: he 'literally glowed; without a word or a gesture of exultation a new well-being radiated from him and filled the small room'.

This is followed by the slow hint, in the next hour or so, that the dream has already started to shatter against reality. Now the irony becomes tragic rather than comic in tone, as Carraway's sympathy veers round towards Gatsby and starts to become engaged. No reality, however great or vital, could have stood up to an illusion on the scale that Gatsby has constructed.

> Almost five years! There must have been moments even that afternoon when Daisy tumbled short of his dreams – not through her own fault, but because of the colossal vitality of his illusion. It had gone beyond her, beyond everything. . . . No amount of fire and freshness can challenge what a man can store up in his ghostly heart.

And Daisy, far from having 'fire and freshness', has only her pale imitation of it. She has grown up in her world of money and carelessness, where 'all night the saxophones wailed the hopeless comment of the Beale Street Blues', and dawn was always an hour of disenchantment. What Gatsby demands of her is that she should go to Tom and say, in all sincerity, 'I never loved you'. This is the unadmirable impossibility upon which his faith is staked; and Carraway's warning to him, as soon as the full extent of the 'rather harrowing' intention becomes clear, is a striking example of the way in which the most elementary commonsense can sometimes knock a man's private world to pieces.

> 'I wouldn't ask too much of her,' I ventured. 'You can't repeat the past.' 'Can't repeat the past?' he cried incredulously. 'Why, of course you can.'

Gatsby has ignored, and disbelieved in, such depressing commonplaces as Carraway's – the depressing commonplaces which are at the heart of Daisy's cynicism, and of the greyness of the ash-grey men. In his own private world past and future can indeed be held captive in the present. His faith allows almost boundless possibilities to be contemplated: and if the 'universe' which has 'spun itself out in his brain' does happen to be one of 'ineffable gaudiness', this does not alter the fact that it is more remarkable, and colourful, than the realities against which it breaks. Like Tamburlaine, Gatsby has made a 'Platonic conception of himself' out of the extravagant emotions and aspirations of an adolescent. Like Tamburlaine too, he has made himself vulnerable by acknowledging the power of a Zenocrate. It is only poetic justice perhaps that his own Zenocrate should turn out to be Daisy. But whoever it had been, the result would have been the same.

The battle between Gatsby and Tom in its prime aspect is the battle between illusion and reality. Tom has the nature of things on his side, and it is part of the nature of things that he and Daisy belong together. Daisy has to say to Gatsby not 'I loved you alone', but 'I loved you too'. This 'too' is Tom's victory, and he can follow it up by equating Gatsby's romance with his own hole-in-the-corner affair with Myrtle, calling it a 'presumptuous little flirtation' and announcing that it is now at an end. After this Gatsby has no weapons left for the fight. He goes on watching over Daisy to the end, but half aware himself now of the annihilating fact that he is watching over nothing. 'So I walked away and left him there standing in the moonlight – watching over nothing.'

He has 'broken up like glass against Tom's hard malice' and for this reason he can now be pitied, since Tom's attitude, though conclusively realistic, is also hard and inhuman and smaller than Gatsby's own. The reality turns out to be less admirable, less human than the fantasy. The events leading to Gatsby's death symbolise very powerfully that his downfall, though inevitable, is by no means an unambiguous triumph of moral powers. His death is brought about by Daisy, who first lets him shield her and then deserts him; by Tom, who directs the demented Wilson to the place where he is to be found; and by Wilson himself – a representative of the ash-grey men who comes to Gatsby in his disillusionment as a terrible embodiment of the realities which have killed his dream.

> Gatsby must have looked up at an unfamiliar sky through frightening leaves and shivered as he found what a grotesque thing a rose is and how raw the sunlight was upon the scarcely created grass. A new world, material without being real, where poor ghosts, breathing dreams like air, drifted fortuitously about . . . like that ashen, fantastic figure gliding towards him through the amorphous trees.

A nightmare of this kind demands some sympathy; and if Dr Eckleburg is unable to provide it, as he looks down unseeingly upon the drama, then there is all the more call for humanity to supply the need. But Gatsby's 'friends' fade away in the hour of death; and Gatsby, whose contribution to his own death has been loyalty to Daisy (the one real and valuable emotion bound up with his fantasy), is left alone at the end.

VII

But not completely alone. His father turns up, with pathetic evidences of Gatsby's youthful aspirations and his generosity as a son; one of the guests who has attended Gatsby's parties attends the funeral; and Carraway himself remains, determined to act in a decently human way. '. . . it grew upon me that I was responsible, because no one else was interested – interested, I mean, with that intense personal interest to which everyone has some vague right in the end.'

Carraway is also by now converted to Gatsby: 'I found myself on Gatsby's side, and alone.' His final compliment to Gatsby, 'They're a rotten crowd. . . . You're worth the whole damn bunch put together', may not add up to much, but it is at least true, and a statement to which everything has been moving. At the very least, it is a recognition that being right about the nature of things is no excuse for being inhuman. In its broader implications, it is part of the larger meaning of the novel: which is that in a tragic and imperfect world scorn and condemnation can often come too easily as attitudes. Human warmth and pity may not be able to set everything to rights; but they are costlier and more decent attitudes than mere judgement, and in the waste land, perhaps juster than judgement itself.

Carraway's befriending of Gatsby is certainly not easy for himself. The cost is symbolised in the ending of his short affair with Jordan Baker. He had been attracted to Jordan in the first place by her self-sufficiency ('Almost any exhibition of complete self-sufficiency draws a stunned tribute from me'), partly by her appearance of 'moral attention' ('She was a slender, small-breasted girl, with an erect carriage, which was accentuated by throwing her body backward to the shoulders like a young cadet') and partly by the needs of his own loneliness. But Jordan turns out, in the end, to be as worthless as the rest: 'moral attention' may be necessary at times in self-defence, but as a total attitude to life it has its limits. Carraway's desire for emotional detachment had, from the start, a certain pessimism underlying it – an acceptance of disenchantment which finds expression in some of the most characteristic of his reflections.

> I was thirty. Before me stretched the portentous, menacing road of a new decade. . . . Thirty – the promise of a decade of loneliness, a thinning list of single men to know, a thinning brief-case of enthusiasm, thinning hair.

He cannot make reality more acceptable than it is, or find a way out of the waste land, or suggest a cure for the cynicism which is eating out the heart of society. He can however prize the highest human values that he sees, and respond to the misfortunes of others with a pity which has in it a feeling for human suffering as a whole. It is characteristic that in the closing sentences he should find in Gatsby's tragic awakening a symbol of the disenchantment of mankind as a whole – and end on a note which, transcending both Gatsby's personal fate, and the *folie de grandeur* of the America which he also represents, achieves a universal and haunting vision:

> As I sat there brooding on the old, unknown world, I thought of Gatsby's wonder when he first picked out the green light at the end of Daisy's dock. He had come a long way to this blue lawn, and his dream must have seemed so close that he could hardly fail to grasp it. He did not know that it was already behind him, somewhere back in that vast obscurity beyond the city, where the dark fields of the republic rolled on under the night.
>
> Gatsby believed in the green light, the orgiastic future that year by year recedes before us. It eluded us then, but that's no matter – tomorrow we will run faster, stretch out our arms further . . . And one fine morning—
>
> So we beat on, boats against the current, borne back ceaselessly into the past.

7 Trial by Enigma: Kafka's *The Trial*

> The Caterpillar and Alice looked at each other for some time in silence: at last the Caterpillar took the hookah out of its mouth, and addressed her in a languid, sleepy voice.
>
> 'Who are *you*?' said the Caterpillar.
>
> This was not an encouraging opening for a conversation. Alice replied, rather shyly, 'I – I hardly know, Sir, just at present – at least I know who I *was* when I got up this morning, but I think I must have been changed several times since then.'
>
> 'What do you mean by that?' said the Caterpillar, sternly. 'Explain yourself!'
>
> 'I can't explain *myself*, I'm afraid, Sir,' said Alice, 'because I'm not myself, you see.'
>
> 'I don't see,' said the Caterpillar.
>
> 'I'm afraid I can't put it more clearly,' Alice replied very politely, 'for I can't understand it myself to begin with; and being so many different sizes in a day is very confusing.'
>
> 'It isn't', said the Caterpillar.
>
> 'Well, perhaps you haven't found it so yet,' said Alice; 'but when you have to turn into a chrysalis – you will some day, you know – and then after that into a butterfly, I should think you'll find it a little queer, won't you?'
>
> 'Not a bit,' said the Caterpillar.
>
> 'Well, perhaps *your* feelings may be different,' said Alice; 'all I know is, it would be very queer to *me*!'
>
> 'You!' said the Caterpillar contemptuously. 'Who are *you*?'

I

In the last four chapters we have moved a long way, it might seem, from *Comus*. Yet is it as far as it looks? The scholar gipsy, the Governess, Aschenbach, Gatsby were all idealists – all Platonists at heart, seeking elusive perfections in their way. If they have become progressively more defeated, or more dangerous, or more tawdry than Milton's Lady, is this due chiefly to an unpropitious setting, or to themselves? Perhaps the world is less propitious to Platonism now, as Arnold imagined; but perhaps the Platonic vision requires virtues that have been eroded by powerful modern trends. It may require a more total renunciation of self and of sensuality than post-romantic men usually understand or aspire to, if the true vision of beauty, goodness and truth is to be seen. Our central figures in the last four chapters have been immersed in romantic demands, egocentric needs, insane visions, which might be at least as much the cause of their malaise as its effect. With Kafka's *The Trial*, we come now to a very distinctively modern experience, at the point where romantic egotism – I shall suggest – finally pushes a man over the abyss.

II

Among the many reflections which spring to mind when reading *The Trial*,[1] I find two that predominate: the first, that whatever it may ultimately 'mean' it is, for me, one of the most important and relevant books of this century, and the second, that it is curiously similar in some ways to *Alice in Wonderland* and *Through the Looking-Glass*. To start from the second of these points, a simple illustration of the similarity might be found in the following extract:

> On his way up he disturbed many children who were playing on the stairs and looked at him angrily as he strode through their ranks. 'If I ever come here again,' he told himself, 'I must either bring sweets to cajole them with or else a stick to beat them.'

The strange and dreamlike quality of the situation (K. has been summoned to his first interrogation, and is searching for the law courts in a block of working-class flats), and the directness and clarity of K.'s logic within the situation, are very reminiscent of Carroll. It may be then that an attempt to compare and contrast Carroll and Kafka will provide one of the many possible approaches that can be made to *The Trial*. This at least will be my hope in what follows.

The undertaking is of course a limited one by its very nature. A large-scale account of Kafka would have, I think, to compare his work with the Book of Job, with *The Divine Comedy*, with

[1] *The Trial*, trans. W. and E. Muir (Secker & Warburg, 1950; available also in Penguin Books).

King Lear, and with other major explorations of man's basic religious problems.[1] What is man, what is value, what are the ways and purposes of God? These are the questions Kafka has chiefly in mind, the questions that make him of major importance as a writer, and clearly they transcend anything that Carroll has consciously in mind when writing his books about Alice. The comparison with Carroll is on a more modest scale therefore than comparison with Dante or Shakespeare would be, and it starts from a similarity in technique rather than from similarity of conscious intention. I fancy, however, that a likeness in technique points also to a likeness in sensibility, and that something more important than the remarking of a stylistic coincidence will be found to be in question.

The Alice books are, first and foremost, children's tales, full of charm and delight, and certainly among the best ever written. They cannot therefore be interpreted as books embodying any conscious exploration of religious problems, and upon this most important difference between Carroll and Kafka I want to insist at the start. When it has been allowed for, however, I think we can go on to say that behind the strange logic of Carroll's nonsense, and the archetypal contours of his dream situations, a pattern of *feeling* may be discerned that is not dissimilar to Kafka's. And it is for this reason, I believe, that Alice is not merely a children's heroine, but one who is perpetually fascinating to adult and mature minds as well. In her travels she proves herself, like Joseph K., an eager seeker for understanding in new and baffling territory. Her meetings with strange characters who tell her conflicting stories and are by no means all well disposed towards her are not unlike K.'s various encounters in *The Trial*. Like all children she is disposed to question everything in the search for logical explanations; and, like Joseph K., she finds that logic, far from clarifying and patterning events, serves very often only to make confusion worse confounded. Like Joseph K. also, she is fated always to be questioning her 'identity'. The conversation with

[1] The comparison with *Pilgrim's Progress* is often made, since both works are religious allegory. But here it should be borne in mind that, whereas Bunyan starts from a dogmatic theology and relates man's spiritual experience to this in concrete allegory, Kafka starts from the enigma of human experience and tries to feel his way from the enigma to its 'meaning', in the medium of complex and flexible symbols.

the Caterpillar at the head of this chapter is wholly typical of
the intellectual life of Wonderland and Looking-Glass Land.

Kafka-like overtones are implicit in Alice's situation; and in so
far as such overtones are unplanned and therefore committed to
no single intended interpretation, they are all the richer in their
wide suggestiveness. The strange room in which Alice finds herself, with many doors to choose from on either side, and at the
end a small door, impossible to pass through, yielding a view on to
the ideal garden beyond, springs to mind at once as an example.
The situation is one that symbolises a great many different, and
not necessarily consistent ideas – the dangers and difficulties of
choice; the insecurity of human experience; the perennial lure of
perfection and of the ideal; the vicissitudes of man's emotional
search for happiness through the ages, or his intellectual search
for truth. Associations such as these are potentially present in such
a situation; they are evoked by it, whether with the conscious consent of the author or not. They make their impact on us as we
read (a subconscious impact until they are brought to the surface
for analysis) and contribute to the sense of significance which a
mature mind finds in Carroll's books. They might be called the
method in his madness, or the imaginative centre of his effect (*if*
to call them this is not to confuse one effect of the books with the
actual purpose of their author).

Most of the situations in *Wonderland* and *Through the Looking-
Glass* are rich in potential associations of this kind. The caucus
race, haphazard, without rules, without beginning or end, culmin-
ating in the verdict 'Everybody has won, and all must have
prizes' (though Alice herself has to give the prizes, since there is
no one else to do so); and the croquet match, with its shifting
arena, dominated by the arbitrary and terrifying judgements of
the Queen of Hearts, ending with the removal of all the players
to be executed (though we later hear that they are not really to
lose their heads – that is only the Queen's 'fancy') – these situations would have suited Kafka. He could have heightened the
emotional intensity, used the evocative quality of the situations
consciously instead of unconsciously, and imported them into his
own pattern of events in *The Trial*.

The trial of the Knave of Hearts, to be more specific, is remarkably like K.'s first interrogation. The atmosphere in the
courtroom is similar – a crowd of unfamiliar and curious people,

all very conscious of Alice in the one case, K. in the other, all responding unpredictably to what is said, all involved in a complex and inexplicable proceeding. The charge against the Knave of Hearts is shrouded in verbal mystery; the evidence is a chaotic jumble; there is a precarious balance between 'important' and 'unimportant', so that in the end one does not know which of these terms is the more applicable; there is a call for the sentence before the verdict and the collapse of the court in the end into meaninglessness:

> 'Off with her head!' the Queen shouted at the top of her voice. Nobody moved.
>   'Who cares for *you*?' said Alice (she had grown to her full size by this time). 'You're nothing but a pack of cards.'

All these things remind us of Kafka; the degree of seriousness is different, but the situation is very like that of K. in *The Trial*.

To list the moments in Carroll when large and often sinister 'meanings' suggest themselves would occupy the rest of this chapter. A few will have to be sufficient. Consider for example the difficulties of life in Looking-Glass Land – where an all-out effort is needed not for progress, but merely to avoid losing ground ('it takes all the running *you* can do, to keep in the same place'); where any likelihood of positive rewards is an illusion existing only in the past or future ('Jam to-morrow and jam yesterday – but never jam today'); where Humpty Dumpty can state the problem of terminology are devastatingly as the most advanced of Logical Positivists ('When *I* use a word,' Humpty Dumpty said, in rather a scornful tone, 'it means just what I choose it to mean – neither more nor less'); where the Oriental pessimism of Tweedledum and Tweedledee can identify Alice's whole existence with the insubstantial dreams of the Red King ('Well, it's no use *your* talking about waking him,' said Tweedledum, 'when you're only one of the things in his dream. You know very well you're not real'); and where Alice can arrive as a Queen at a feast given in her honour, only to be received as a stranger and intruder. All these difficulties about life in Looking-Glass Land at least suggest, in their concrete and profound symbolism, some of the most abiding and disturbing crises in our human lot.

Alice is logical in her questionings, but the dream is too complex, too shifting, too enigmatic, to be plumbed by her logic. She cannot find a system into which it all fits; she cannot cram her Wonderland and Looking-Glass Land into a simple pattern. Bafflement of this kind is the experience also of Joseph K., and is at the core of the comparison I am trying to make. K., like Alice, is in a strange and enigmatic situation; he is tried by enigma, and he cannot understand his experience; he cannot reduce it to a pattern.

In Carroll the overtones of his situations are incidental; in Kafka they are intended, and constitute a religious exploration of reality. The method which Carroll hit upon by accident, and without fully understanding its implications, is used deliberately and with conscious artistry by Kafka. The situations are meant to be meaningful, and their meaning is precisely the impossibility of grasping by logic what the meanings are. As in Carroll, in other words, there is no simple or limiting 'interpretation' of the situations in which K. finds himself, no single allegorical intention of the type we find in Bunyan. But whereas in Carroll the overtones are incidental to a pleasant and enthralling tale, in Kafka they are at the very core of what he is doing. They amount to a profound, and profoundly disturbing, vision of human life.

III

Someone must have been telling lies about Joseph K., for without having done anything wrong he was arrested one fine morning.

So *The Trial* begins, and we are plunged into the essential mystery. Who has been telling lies, what lies have been told, and why? The unwary reader might suppose that this riddle will be resolved as he reads on, but actually, the clearest statement that he is likely to find has already been made. The situation is presented clearly enough – an arrest, with its problems of who has ordered the arrest, and why, and on what pretext. But the answers to such questions, though K. seeks them single-mindedly and with all his faculties as a man, recede, and blur, and dissolve as he grasps for them. His greatest need is to understand, and this is no mere academic need, it is one on which his very life depends. Though he searches, however with his mind, he discovers only new problems, new difficulty, new levels of enigma. The situation grows around him, absorbs him, moves him further and further away from the everyday world of normality. In that world men may live by convention, think little, and have the illusion, at least, of knowing what they are doing and why they are doing it. But for K. the commonplace world is stripped away. He is torn from the pattern of an ordered society, where familiarity with things is mistaken for understanding of them and security is to be found in an accepted and unquestioned body of convention, and plunged into a position where he finds himself alone and isolated, not knowing the rules, not knowing if there are any rules; life itself at stake, and no 'path or friendly clue' to be his guide.

At first, after the arrest, he still thinks in familiar terms – it is a practical joke, a mistake; it can be settled by a few words with an intelligent man, or by the production of some relevant documents. Only gradually does he come to realise how completely the arrest has destroyed the pattern of his past existence, and thrown him into a place where no assumption is safe, no technique works, no person can be trusted, no development can be 'placed' or understood. His subsequent attempts to make the universe rational and safe again are all so many types of failure. His sense of insecurity and unreality increases as the unanswerability of fundamental questions becomes clear.

'The thought of his case never left him now.' Analysis of the situation turns out, often enough, to be analysis of his relationships with other people, and this, in turn, to be a branch of self-analysis. 'To ask questions was surely the main thing.' But what questions? That, in itself, is a puzzle. Continuous intellectual activity leading away from, not towards, understanding – this state, which the medieval (and Miltonic) world considered to be a prerogative of Lucifer, is the one in which K., as a modern man in search of religious truth, finds himself involved. Moments of clarity, when a logical pattern seems on the point of emerging from the chaos, always lead him on to betrayal. During his first interrogation, for example, he addresses the officials present – and as he does so, emboldened to attack them for injustice, he gathers confidence for a moment from the clichés that start to come.

> There can be no doubt that behind all the actions of this court . . . a great organisation at work. . . . An organisation which . . . employs corrupt warders, stupid inspectors . . .

innocent persons accused of guilt . . . innocent men humiliated
in the presence of public assemblies . . .

For a moment the situation is generalised, simplified to the clearly
defined formula of innocence as the victim of corruption. K. forgets his own involvement, slips back into the confidence of an
everyday frame of reference, takes refuge from reality behind a
familiar routine of rhetoric, speaks in the manner of one writing
a protest to a daily paper. But, as he speaks, the audience begin to
react strangely, he is aware of mounting hostility, he realises that
he may have made a fatal miscalculation, the nightmare uncertainty beyond and around his logic reasserts itself. What is he
really talking about? What are his premises? Who is he talking
to? What is he really doing here? Logic stumbles and breaks
against these unanswerable riddles; he is talking in a vacuum,
using words that had a meaning once, but have no longer that
meaning now. The framework of cliché and stock response, simple
hypothesis and simple judgement, has broken up, it has been
utterly discredited. There can be no possibility of a return to it.

K.'s uncertainty relates especially to his relationships. Even the
most familiar people become bewildering and inaccessible – his
landlady, his neighbour, his colleagues at the bank. They speak
and act as they used to, but do they mean what they seem to
mean? The court officials are at the root of the enigma. K. does
not even know whether they are friends or enemies. There is
evidence for both views; to commit himself to one of them would
be to simplify, not so to commit himself is to risk making the most
frightful of errors. They can, he knows, seem to be courteous,
conscientious, hard-working. They take pains to explain to him
about the 'higher powers'; and if their explanations merely in-
crease the number of things that need to be explained, can this
be urged against them as their fault? But, on the other hand, their
friendliness may be the merest façade. It may be that they have
no authority to speak, or are misinformed when they do. Their
very offers to help may be only a 'cat-and-mouse' game, a diabolical delight in his weakness. 'Was the Advocate seeking to
comfort him or to drive him to despair? He could not tell.'

This insecurity is mirrored in his relationship with Fräulein
Bürstner. The situation between them starts simply enough, but
almost out of nothing complexities develop, or are assumed to
have developed, that defy analysis. K. comes to a point where he

is talking in riddles to Fräulein Bürstner's friend, who acts as an intermediary between them – every word making the situation less tangible, and yet the very fact that they are talking about it in such a way establishing the fact that there is a complex situation to be dealt with. 'His relationship with Fräulein Bürstner seemed to fluctuate with the case itself.' Here, as elsewhere in the book, the image of a labyrinth becomes the controlling one. The mind looses its way, is defeated:

> Things fall apart; the centre cannot hold;
> Mere anarchy is loosed upon the world.

A microcosm of this aspect of the work occurs in the penultimate chapter of the book as we have it, 'In the Cathedral'. A priest calls K. by name and, having secured his attention, tells him the following parable:

> . . . before the Law stands a door-keeper on guard. To this door-keeper there comes a man from the country who begs for admittance to the Law. But the door-keeper says that he cannot admit the man at the moment. The man, on reflection, asks if he will be allowed, then, to enter later. 'It is possible,' answers the door-keeper, 'but not at this moment.' Since the door leading into the Law stands open as usual and the door-keeper steps to one side, the man bends down to peer through the entrance. When the door-keeper sees that, he laughs and says: 'If you are so strongly tempted, try to get in without my permission. But note that I am powerful. And I am only the lowest door-keeper. From hall to hall, keepers stand at every door, one more powerful than the other. Even the third of these has an aspect that even I cannot bear to look at.' These are difficulties which the man from the country has not expected to meet, the Law, he thinks, should be accessible to every man and at all times, and when he looks more closely at the door-keeper in his furred robe, with his huge pointed nose and long thin, Tartar beard, he decides that he had better wait until he gets permission to enter. The door-keeper gives him a stool and lets him sit down at the side of the door. There he sits waiting for days and years. He makes many attempts to be allowed in and wearies the door-keeper with his importunity. The door-keeper often engages him in brief conversation, asking him about his home and about other matters, but the questions are put quite impersonally, as great men put questions, and always conclude with the statement that the

man cannot be allowed to enter yet. The man, who has equipped himself with many things for his journey, parts with all he has, however valuable, in the hope of bribing the door-keeper. The door-keeper accepts it all, saying, however, as he takes each gift: 'I take this only to keep you from feeling that you have left something undone.' During all these long years the man watches the door-keeper almost incessantly. He forgets about the other door-keepers, and this one seems to him the only barrier between himself and the Law. In the first years he curses his evil fate aloud; later, as he grows old, he only mutters to himself. He grows childish, and since in his prolonged watch he has learned to know even the fleas in the door-keeper's fur collar, he begs the very fleas to help him and to persuade the door-keeper to change his mind. Finally his eyes grow dim and he does not know whether the world is really darkening around him or whether his eyes are only deceiving him. But in the darkness he can now perceive a radiance that streams immortally from the door of the Law. Now his life is drawing to a close. Before he dies, all that he has experienced during the whole time of his sojourn condenses in his mind into one question, which he has never yet put to the door-keeper. He beckons the door-keeper, since he can no longer raise his stiffening body. The door-keeper has to bend far down to hear him, for the difference in size between them has increased very much to the man's disadvantage. 'What do you want to know now?' asks the door-keeper, 'you are insatiable.' 'Everyone strives to attain the Law,' answers the man, 'how does it come about, then, that in all these years no one has come seeking admittance but me?' The door-keeper perceives that the man is at the end of his strength and his hearing is failing, so he bellows in his ear: 'No one but you could gain admittance through this door, since this door was intended only for you. I am now going to shut it.'

K.'s immediate reaction, as always, is an attempt to analyse the parable. In its literal meaning, it tells the story of one man's search for the truth, including the mysterious answers and glimpses which he seems to have revealed to him, and the apparent ironic injustice of the fate he eventually meets. In its relation to K. as he attempts to understand it, the parable as a whole stands for the data provided to the human mind by its experience of life. It is described by the Priest as 'scripture', be-cause every word of it is part of the evidence that the mind has to work on, and nothing therefore can be ignored. K.'s efforts to elucidate the parable's 'meaning', like that of other 'commentators' whom the Priest mentions, are inspired by a desire for intellectual clarification. He searches for some key principle, some simple explanation of the door-keeper's relationship to the man from the country, which will make sense of everything that happens. Every hypothesis he tries, however, turns out to be incomplete, in that it leaves some aspect of the parable unaccounted for. The function of the Priest, who stands for something not unlike Intellectual Integrity, is to point every time to the aspects of the parable that do not fit in with K.'s hypothesis, and to insist upon the sacredness of 'scripture'. Anyone, he implies, can formulate some sort of theory, but only a theory covering all the facts is finally of any value, and this is exactly what logic, if K. is ruthlessly honest, cannot provide.

The outlines of the 'meaning' of the parable seem clear enough. The man from the country is the human pilgrim, engaged on his search for truth. The door-keeper is in some sense the theory or philosophy or religion which he finds, and accepts as his authority. The result of their encounter is that the man seems in the end to have been betrayed. His life has passed away in waste and unfulfilment, because he is either misinformed of the truth or has misunderstood it; and this because the door-keeper is either deliberately lying, or because he does not have the authority he claims, or because he does represent an authority but the authority is too strange to be understood.

Each time K. proposes a theory, the Priest points out defects in terms of the actual wording of the parable. His technique is that of the fundamentalist interpretation of scripture, but it is turned upon the data of life itself. The Priest insists that his business is not to provide an hypothesis of his own, but to bear constant witness to the evidence.

> I am only showing you the various opinions concerning that point [he tells K. at one stage]. You must not pay too much attention to them. The scriptures are unalterable, and the comments often enough merely express the commentators' bewilderment.

K., defeated in his various attempts to elucidate, drops at last into silence.

He was too tired to survey all the conclusions arising from the
story, and the trains of thought into which it was leading him
were unfamiliar, dealing with impalpabilities better suited to a
theme for discussion among Court Officials than for him. The
simple story had lost its clear outline; he wanted to put it out
of his mind.

This exhaustion may well remind us of a similar remark that
occurs earlier in *The Trial*.

You must remember [K. is told] that in these courts things are
always coming up for discussion that are simply beyond reason;
people are too tired and distracted to think and so they take
refuge in superstition.

'Superstition,' in this context, seems a term wide enough to cover
any dogmatism, any convention, any *Weltanschauung*, however
large or internally coherent it might be.

IV

I want now to return to the comparison and contrast with Lewis
Carroll, in order to find a centre for these comments.

Right up to the end of the nineteenth century, many moral
beliefs remained unchallenged by society at large. The breakdown
of traditional faith had gone a long way, Matthew Arnold had
heard the sea of faith retreating with a 'melancholy, long withdrawing roar', but morality, at least, was much as it was. Indeed,
many Victorians imagined that the sterner moral commitments
were self-evident, and used them to belabour the religion which
had in fact created them and made them prevail. Arnold himself
was also clear that the Church of England must at all costs be
preserved and continued – modified (of course) in its actual theology, but kept alive as an essential guardian and dispenser of
sweetness and light.

Lewis Carroll was near enough to a tradition of intellectual
agnosticism to feel that all things had been called in doubt, but
not near enough to it perhaps to take the possibility of a complete
breakdown of moral and social certainties seriously. He was near
enough to it to know all the disturbing questions that could be
asked, but not near enough to believe that the questions might
end by destroying European civilisation itself. The more anarchic

suggestions of, say, Humpty Dumpty concerning 'language', or of Tweedledum concerning Alice's 'reality' were still, to him, strictly speaking, *nonsense*. They could be played with by his keenly logical mind, and used in the creation of a make-believe world for children, but they were not yet in danger of becoming *sense*, and in so doing, of threatening the very foundations of social sanity and order.

Alice, it will be noticed, is in no ways neurotic; she does not feel guilty, or hunted, or persecuted. Not even the most determined exponents of abnormal psychology could make her anything other than she is, a normal, happy, and essentially delightful little girl. 'But I'm *not* a serpent, I tell you,' she says to the Pigeon and we have no cause to doubt her. She is sometimes frightened a little, usually perplexed, and even made to cry a little on occasions; but throughout her trial by enigma she never loses her dignity and is always equal to the Queen of Hearts and the other alarming figures she meets. In the end she wakes up to sanity and finds the people of her dreams only a pack of cards after all.

The total feeling of Carroll's books is different, in short, from the feeling of Kafka's. And in view of the similarity of the archetypal patterns in both, this difference seems to me worthy of comment. The adventures which Alice meets with are pleasant adventures, and the characters she meets are basically pleasant characters. Generations of children have found them to be so at any rate, and in this matter no surer critics could be found. The very perplexities that Alice meet with are a source of pleasure to her as she teases her mind with them, and not a cause of pain. In the background of her adventures, also, order rather than chaos is to be discerned. In Looking-Glass Land the order is that appropriate to a game of chess, with something, too, of the feeling of a game of chess – where problems occur, but inside the framework of known rules, and the solving of them is no more than a pleasant academic exercise for the intellect. (Alice herself, of course, does not know the 'rules', but Lewis Carroll, her creator, does.) In the last analysis, the Alice books are healthy and sane and satisfying in their effect; the experience of reading them is nothing like the experience of reading Kafka.

All of this may be only another way of saying that Carroll's work is intended for the pleasure of children, and is not in any sense a religious allegory. Nevertheless, in view of their potentially

Kafkaesque situations, which could so easily have taken on disquieting overtones had Carroll been less securely rooted in Christian values than he was, a tentative generalisation might perhaps be risked. For Carroll, the topsy-turvy world he created was a welcome escape from the everyday world. Just because the order and sanity of Victorian England was everywhere accepted, he could afford to delight in puzzlement and the reversal of normality as a relief from stern reality. The symbolic situations of Wonderland and Looking-Glass Land were no more than fantasy to him. This is why he was unaware of their potential for real despair.

It is not until we come to our own century, with its fragmentation of culture, its religious and moral doubts, and its final breakdown of any remnants of a *Weltanschauung* that can be said to be generally accepted, that similar symbolic situations turn from charming nonsense to sinister sense.

V

The situation of K. in *The Trial* is an embodiment of Kafka's own sensitive and troubled search for religious truth. I have said enough to indicate my own high opinion of it, and should like, before making a personal assessment, to defend it against two charges that are often made. The first of these is that K. is not a representative man at all but a neurotic, and that his predicament can be regarded more properly as a department of morbid psychology than as a profound religious allegory. In support of this indictment, it can be pointed out that K. has a decided persecution complex, that he has an unhealthy consciousness of anxiety arising from the circumstances of his arrest, and that his moral and intellectual values diverge further and further as the trial proceeds from those of normal everyday 'common sense'. He is moreover emotionally unstable, and his moods of elation and despair arise from chance encounters or associations of ideas rather than from any rational causes or coherent trains of thought.

There is of course an element of truth in this; but to conclude on these grounds alone that K. is a neurotic is to ignore the events that happen to him in the book. Unless the extreme view is taken that his 'trial' is entirely a subjective fantasy, we have to admit that his feelings of persecution and guilt are not unrelated to an adequate external cause. He would be a psychopathic 'case' only if his feelings arose groundlessly. Since they are related to an actual situation, and are by no means psychologically inappropriate to it, there is no evidence for concluding that he is seriously abnormal.

We have cause in our own time to know that ordeals like that to which K. is subjected, and the emotions to which they necessarily give rise, are by no means reserved for the mentally unbalanced. The machinery of ordinary legal proceedings, and of ordinary bureaucratic proceedings, are perplexing enough to the average man. The law courts in *Bleak House* and the circumlocution office in *Little Dorrit* should not be forgotten when reading Kafka. More than this, the ordeal by inquisition, by Gestapo, by concentration camp, can break men down in much the way that K. is broken. It is no new thing for an individual to find himself helplessly at the mercy of a vast, and hostile, and morally inexplicable machine.

Even on the political level then (which in *The Trial* is the level on which the literal meaning moves), we must allow that K.'s emotions are in great part accounted for by his situation, and that the situation is one that remains permanently possible for us all. The most important meaning, however, is the allegorical one, and here, unless religious experience is thought to be wholly a subjective illusion, we must again allow the appropriateness of K.'s emotions. At this level, he is Everyman face to face with the enigma of the universe – 'Everyman,' that is to say, faced with the doubt, perplexity and fear of our times. As Everyman, he is on trial before a tribunal whose very rules and requirements and nature are, to him, of the most inscrutable kind.

To assert this is not to deny that K., and his creator Kafka, belong to a minority temperament, and are perhaps more continuously and even unhealthily preoccupied with religious problems than the generality of mankind. It is, however, to assert that the problems dealt with in *The Trial* are real, and not imaginary, and of the kind which no sensitive man can evade. It is to assert also that Kafka's mood, even though it is a personal and perhaps a specialised one, manages at the same time to be the mood of a whole generation. In expressing psychological truths about himself, he was expressing imaginative truths about the dilemma of modern man. The malaise of K. is not that of one man only; it is a malaise of the spirit and understanding of the twentieth century. This, therefore, is the true 'centrality' of *The Trial*; and this is the reason why it will remain an important imaginative document of the human spirit even when the spiritual crisis of the age which produced it has passed.

VI

What, then, is this malaise? Kafka nowhere defines it; but I have come to feel that the key insight is moral and relates, perhaps surprisingly, to the hero's character. Instinctively, no doubt, we are on Joseph K.'s side, through the kind of self-identification prompted by fear. But as soon as we think of him objectively, it is clear that he is a somewhat unpleasant man, selfish and lustful, petty and vain. He responds to his inferiors at every point in the novel with arrogance, aping the court officials whenever he can. There is nothing in him of human generosity or religious vision; he has no natural or supernatural resources against the charge of 'guilt'. In this, his mentality colours events, contributing more to the nightmare than at first we might suspect.

To see this is to notice, among the constructional feature of *The Trial*, the oddity of our relationship with K. In *The Turn of the Screw* we are engulfed in the narrator's vision and allowed 'out' only through the most oblique hints. In *Death in Venice* we are close to the hero's consciousness but not contained in it, and free to respond simultaneously as if from within and without. *The Great Gatsby*, on the other hand, presents its hero through a narrator who is in the first place hostile to him and later partially on his side, but each time for reasons strongly personal to himself. *The Trial* might seem closer in this aspect to James than to Mann or Fitzgerald, but the total effect is not really like that of James. Though the narration keeps very close indeed to K.'s consciousness, there is a curious – almost Brechtian – alienation effect. Despite our empathy with K., based on fear of his predicament, there is a continuing neutrality of tone. Just at times the narrator's reflections depart from K.; but always they leave the reader considerable freedom to judge. It is true, no doubt, that the freedom is qualified, much as it is in a strong and compulsive dream. But we are aware of moral defects in K. right from the start, and these become part of our awareness of the trial itself. It is not, I have urged, that he seems mad in the manner of James's Governess, but rather as if his mind is a kind of distorting glass. The Governess seems mad partly because, if we escape her vigilance and imagine the real situation, it is to realise that madness explains things more normally, and more entirely, than ghosts. But K.'s situation is too allegorical to be imagined apart from him: it has to be seen rather as the background to his search for 'truth'. It has to be seen as the mind's probing of a religious predicament: and when it is, a dramatic new perspective appears. May not the most significant aspect be, after all, K.'s refusal of guilt: his willingness to believe almost anything except that the charge against him is true? He is accused of guilt by powers far greater than himself, and traditionally reverenced by all Jewish, Christian and Hellenic minds. In the Old Testament man confronts a holy God in judgement, and knows himself degraded and lost. He calls upon God *de profundis*, loving the Law, but broken under its yoke:

> I am counted as one of them that go down into the pit: and I have been even as a man that hath no strength.
> Free among the dead, like unto them that are wounded, and lie in the grave: who are out of remembrance, and are cut away from thy hand.
> Thou hast laid me in the lowest pit: in a place of darkness, and in the deep.
> Thine indignation lieth hard upon me: and thou hast vexed me with all thy storms.
> Thou hast put away mine acquaintance far from me: and made me to be abhorred of them.
> I am so fast in prison: that I cannot get forth.
> My sight faileth for very trouble: Lord, I have called daily upon thee, I have stretched forth my hands unto thee.
> Dost thou shew wonders among the dead: or shall the dead rise up again, and praise thee?
> Shall thy loving-kindness be shewed in the grave: or thy faithfulness in destruction?
> Shall thy wondrous works be known in the dark: and thy righteousness in the land where all things are forgotten?
> (Psalm lxxxviii 3–12; Coverdale translation)

This consciousness is not peculiar to the Talmud (which certainly influenced Kafka), but pervades every part of the Jewish revelation. And we find it also in Plato, and in St Paul – this sense that man moves in the world as an alienated being, cut off from his true life, yet as much the agent of his catastrophe as its victim. The New Testament calls upon men to know themselves under the aspects of Sin, of Righteousness and of Judgement; and this knowledge has always been the path by which European man has reasserted his dignity, saved his sanity, when tempted to deny beauty, holiness, God from the depth of despair. It is the man who knows himself vile and accepts guilt who is able to live again.

With this in mind it is possible to feel that one of our distinctively modern disasters – closely allied to the refusal of love, which I discussed in connection with *Death in Venice* – is the refusal of guilt. Increasingly in the past one hundred and fifty years, the traditional wisdom and realism of Europe has been replaced by an egocentric and essentially brutish philosophy, deriving immediately from Rousseau and the English and European romantics, but with more distant roots of course in the past. This tradition has chosen, with considerable irony, to see man as 'naturally' good and holy, and to attribute his sufferings and misfortunes to the malign effects of 'society', or civilisation, or impersonal fate. From the start there was an antinomian tendency, discernible in the conversion first of pride, then of envy, anger, lust and other deadly sins, into qualities extolled as virtues and turned into the springs of personal and political life. With the blame for suffering and misfortune placed firmly outside an individual's responsibility, the human heart has asserted its innocence even in outrages, and denied the holiness and judgement of the Word. The quest for ever new freedoms from guilt and judgement has led to the proclamation of anarchy and eroticism as aspects of innocence, and more recently to a 'culture' obsessed with the denial of reason and indeed existence itself, through drugs. The rejection of sin and guilt has turned out to be a rejection of sanity – a positive courting of absurdity, negation and despair. It is a characteristic also of the diseased romantic imagination to interpret its very sufferings existentially – which is to say, still within the prison of the self. The attempt to centre all reality on 'self' has made of 'self' a labyrinth, of the kind nowhere more perfectly imaged, perhaps, than in *The Trial*. The pursuit of impossible 'freedoms', the anarchy of irreligion, is the circumference surrounding and then destroying Joseph K.

What has been rejected, along with the charge of guilt, is the whole Jewish and Christian awareness that man is everywhere confronted with powers greater than himself. These powers were seen as great and good, beautiful and healing, as well as terrible: and terrible only because of the reality of guilt. Man was free to rejoice in the goodness and holiness all around him, to feel their call on his nature, to know them – if guilt could be purged – as his home. It is this older tradition which produced many aspects of sanity and civilisation which, as romanticism has flourished, have gone everywhere into retreat. Romanticism has indeed been the experimental discovery on a grand scale of the old truth, that if a man tries to live as a god, making himself the measure of good and evil, he plunges into the prison-house traditionally known as hell.

The romantic cult of self has turned out to be the annihilation of self, the reversed image of that great truth that a man must die unto himself to live. The 'self' has sought fulfilments in excesses that can only destroy it, if only through the loss of vision to the prior truths outside. The path which begins with the denial of the presence of God and of God's Law in the world ends in sensuality, madness, torment, precisely as Milton in *Comus* showed. In the intervening poem and three tales, we have encountered the working out of the rejection of the older tradition through a number of consciousnesses, all reaping madness and frustration in various ways. The extreme image, I suggest, is Joseph K., whose refusal of guilt, and so of reality, is the labyrinth in which he moves. In refusing to accept the validity of his trial, he trivialises as well as loses himself. The moral squalor of the man is typical of many romantic heroes in modern literature, as they lament their sufferings from progressively more reduced and more brutalised 'selves'. Intelligence endlessly active, endlessly cut off from salvation and insight: surely Milton and his tradition were right to see in this the geography of Hell? To look around one today at the 'progressive' modern consciousness is to see men and women claiming to achieve criticism by rejecting reason, to achieve creativity by rejecting order, to achieve individuality by embracing the mob. The first of our six works again provides the exact analysis:

And they, so perfect is their misery,
Not once perceive their foul disfigurement,
But boast themselves more comely than before . . .

What we find in *The Trial* is not the assertion that there is no salvation, but a demonstration that intellect, imprisoned in self, can never save. If we accept K.'s own version of himself as victim of injustice, we make the error which has more than any other seduced our modern world. In this, *The Trial* bears oblique witness to the old religious truth, that only when a man makes the last tribute from his violated self to beauty and goodness, calling upon God out of the deep, can the prison doors be unlocked. K. never comes to this point and dies in his uncertainty, a typically modern man to the end.

VII

The charge sometimes brought against Kafka is that his work is a hindrance, not a help, to faith. As we know, Kafka himself had doubts on this score, and left orders for the bulk of his writings, including *The Trial*, to be destroyed. Max Brod writes in this connection: 'He would not admit the argument that his work might help other seekers for faith, naturalness and spiritual wholeness, being himself too earnestly and implacably a seeker for the right way of living to feel that he could advise others when his first need was to advise himself.' Doubts of this kind are natural enough in a writer, but we should be ill-advised to take them over uncritically. Kafka's implication in the enigma of existence is sacrificial, in that he offers a total image of modern perplexity without forcing it into a mould of his own. He nowhere implies that there is no truth for K. to find, or indeed that he has no means of finding it; he merely shows K.'s complex failure to find the truth in fact. He does not say that the powers who try K. are evil, or unapproachable, or non-existent, but only that they are enigmatic, and that they can appear to be any of these things. In this, he is no more irreligious than Sophocles is in *Oedipus Rex* and Shakespeare in *King Lear*. He is merely being realistic: and with a realism that religion and irreligion ignore at their peril. If the limitation of unaided human intellect is asserted, this is no more than a scepticism wholly endorsed by minds such as St Augustine's and St Paul's. The exploration allows us to see, however, that doctrinaire agnosticism of the Victorian kind is itself a by-product of romanticism: a willingness of the imprisoned self to reject guilt and enigma which turned out to have peculiarly ironic, as well as arid, effects.

The religious objections to *The Trial* are, to my mind, unfounded; it seems truer to suggest that situations and images similar to those which, for Lewis Carroll, were the stuff of amiable nonsense, are turned by Kafka into one of the profoundest explorations of our modern malaise.

8 Eagles and Trumpets: *The Transmuted Experience of Literature*

It's a very odd thing –
  As odd as can be –
That whatever Miss T. eats
  Turns into Miss T.

Walter de la Mare

Stone, bronze, stone, steel, stone, oakleaves, horses' heels
Over the paving.
And the flags. And the trumpets. And so many eagles.
How many? Count them. And such a press of people.
We hardly knew ourselves that day, or knew the City.
This is the way to the temple, and we so many crowding
  the way.
So many waiting, how many waiting? what did it
  matter on such a day?
Are they coming? No, not yet. You can see some eagles.
  And hear the trumpets.

T. S. Eliot

I

The foregoing chapters have been concerned with particular works of literature, in the terms central to them, and have touched only contingently on form. This chapter might be appended to almost any as a coda, since it seeks to isolate a matter of general application to the literary art. What I want to explore in fact is this: none of the rich emotions aroused in us by literature or drama exactly resembles the appropriate emotion in our lives. The emotions in art are always subtly transmuted, not necessarily towards greater complexities, but towards complexities of a distinctive kind. It is as though the worlds of life and art run parallel, always close, always reflecting each other, never joined.

First, consider a man who slips on a banana skin. In life, some people laugh at him, and some are sympathetic. A lot depends on whether he is hurt. But in the theatre, our responses relate directly to the total context. We know that the actor is not really being hurt, and this is basic. Why waste sympathy on the tumbles of Laurel and Hardy? We are released into enjoyment, and into whatever emotional catharsis such enjoyment brings. Certainly there is no call to rescue the actors on the stage.

This is the first and basic difference between life and art, that art is imitation and, however 'real' the imitation, our response is conditioned by the status we know it to have. In the theatre we contemplate the action from our seats, in our homes we contemplate the pages of a book. Perhaps in the theatre a man may be so carried away by *Othello* that he jumps up to shout warnings or abuse. But what reader of *Oliver Twist* ever shouted warnings at the hero, or imagined that there could be any appeal against the rigorous predestination of Dickens's art? Only a very unsophisticated person could mistake imitation for reality in the theatre. In the study, no one could make this mistake at all.

II

The first difference between life and art is this fact of mimesis; the second is the difference of intensity from one work to another with which the illusion of 'reality' is evoked. Partly, this is to do with the greatness of the writer: naturally Tolstoy's people seem more real than Ethel M. Dell's. But partly too it is a matter of genre. Many works of literature – especially those written before the twentieth century and in forms other than the novel – were conceived in a genre, which by definition implied patterning of material and a particular tone. In farce, for instance, no illusion of 'reality' is attempted; the whole art is to insulate people and their predicaments from the range of sympathy and moral concern. The same to an almost equal degree is true of melodrama, which is distanced from tragedy much as farce is distanced from the comic mode. In farce and melodrama, therefore, a man might slip on a banana skin without arousing any 'natural' concern for his fate. Indeed if we do feel concerned, the art has failed, by developing just the degree of realism which it has to exclude. In farce, we expect to be amused, and anything justifies this; in melodrama it is always right for the villain to be foiled.

These are extreme instances, but what of comedy? Here we move perceptibly closer to 'life'. The illusion of moral realism becomes part of the art, and laughter relates not to a world of its own, but to moral concerns. Jane Austen's heroines live in a world devoted to fitness, so that any accidents happening to them must relate to the whole. In comedy, the man who slips on a banana skin might still then amuse us, but no longer as an end in himself. We shall now most probably feel involved with him as a fellow mortal, in the area of moral judgement suspended between 'He'll be all the better for this' and 'It serves him right'. Yet the expectation of a happy ending absolves us from ruthlessness: this is nothing like laughing at the misfortunes of someone we 'know'.

When we move on to tragedy, simple accidents are no longer possible: Hamlet slipping on a banana skin would destroy the play. This is one of the many possibilities for a man in real experience which is rigidly excluded by the prescriptions of genre. An epic hero of course is still more protected from trivial mishaps, since he exists to celebrate the dignity and triumph of the race.

It may be objected that I am speaking here of pure genre, and that most great literature turns its back on this. Nevertheless, any extension of realism and complexity in art has its own decorum: if the tragic hero slips on a banana skin the play becomes tragicomedy, and this in turn has laws of texture and tone. Perhaps to restate the argument in terms of texture and tone might make it more familiar, since these are recognised bridges between raw experience and literary form. It is worth remembering, however, that just as many older works departed from their genre to play games with it, so many modern works are apt to flirt with genre for similar effects. *The Rape of the Lock* is as complex in the first of these directions as *The Waste Land* is in the second, and neither poem can be rightly understood if genre is ignored.

My first example was a man slipping on a banana skin; my next is a tragic death. Just as a trivial accident is inappropriate to tragedy and epic, so is tragic death to comedy and farce. The art of tragedy is to create a high illusion of reality, and to establish empathy; the classic emotions of pity and fear are aroused, and cast out. If there are comic interludes, these will merely heighten the tragedy by counterpointing with suffering those kinds of irony or absurdity which move us most.

III

In many great tragedies, it is true, we are taken beyond a sense of the hero's personal identity to his archetypal role as sacrificial victim, fisher king or dying god; and this, to some degree, modifies response. But such suggestions do not subtract from personal involvement though they may enrich it: certainly we suffer with Desdemona in the murder scene as with a fellow mortal, even while we respond to the profoundly ironic vision of victim and priest.

What does transmute our personal involvement, and again very basically, is that Othello and Desdemona are not our own friends or relations in 'life'. And here I return to the most basic matter of mimesis, the inevitable distinction between people created — however powerfully — in a fiction or drama, and the people continually present in our own hearts and homes. We don't, after all, 'know' Othello and Desdemona as people; we haven't lived with them, and their death leaves no gap in our lives. As heroes of literature, indeed, they have their own immortality, beyond even the author who gave them birth. Where now, one asks, are Joseph K. and Aschenbach? And there they are, waiting for us, and for those who come after, to reach them once again from the shelves. There, in the marvellous antechamber of drama, Othello is waiting, for the next great actor who will bring him to life. Our relationship with these people is based on a fundamental aesthetic paradox; they are both more real, and less real, to us in their triumphs and sufferings, than are many of the people we 'know'. More real, because it is the art of the writer to make them so. 'He is a man', says Arthur Miller of his hero, 'and he is suffering. So attention must be paid. Attention, attention must be paid to such a man.' And we pay attention, more than we normally give to our family or neighbours, as the writer dissolves our complacency, our insensitivity, our escapism, in the salutary corrosive of art. Yet his people are not our people before the curtain rises, and they are ours only fitfully after the two-hour traffic of our stage. This may explain, I think, the somewhat exaggerated grief and indignation with which the deaths of characters in a long-running serial are apt to be greeted. For many people, the Archers or the Coronation Street crew are a daily experience. To this extent their deaths do leave a gap in their audience's lives.

I am dealing here with the very obvious, yet with factors so obvious that they can all too readily be overlooked. We don't *know* the people in literature and drama in the sense of emotionally depending upon them; and this produces other important transmutations between 'life' and 'art'. Our response to all fictional characters, for instance, is founded on interest in them; and on interest in them not only as people, but as pieces in their particular aesthetic game. We are just as interested in the fool or bore, or very nearly, as we are in the hero or wit. By the same token, we are protected from fictional characters, including the villains; we have nothing personal to hope or fear from Cleopatra, or Becky Sharp, or Madame Merle. When we seem to be personally affected, it is on account of what they evoke in us. The artist borrows our hopes and fears, our personal experience, to clothe his illusions – to deck them with as rich and royal a cloth as he can aspire us to provide. But evocation is still at one stage removed from daily experience. We are involved rather by the increased sense of stimulation of our own potential than by something directly operative in our lives. If we are living through events close to those we read of, or if we feel a fictional character illuminates someone we know, or if some deep-seated tendency in our own nature is played upon, or some ruling passion or interest excited – *then* our interest might spill over from art to life. But this is still at one remove from reality: and it poses dangers of distorted reading against which, as trained critics, we especially guard. It is only very specialised and peripheral literature which directly affects us: pornography when it acts as an aphrodisiac, horror stories when they leave us afraid to go to bed.

IV

The central perception in such comments is that art is contemplation rather than action; it invites us to be profoundly moved by humanity, but in a medium where there is no direct call to intervene. I say this in full knowledge of the reservations which are immediately needed. Contemplation may be opposed to participation, but it is nothing like indolence; the extended consciousness offered by literature is not laid aside with the book.

Like all meaningful contemplation, it challenges us to become fuller people. There remain, however, the differences between the act of contemplation itself and its active consequences, which I would like to summarise in a convenient form:

   (i) All art re-enacts rather than enacts; it is nearer to the Mass this morning than to Calvary two thousand years ago.

  (ii) All art calls upon us to imagine, and to contemplate, and to recreate; not to participate, not to go into immediate action, not to create.

 (iii) The art of literature tugs experience in certain genre directions, and these presuppose differing degrees of 'realism' in the illusion they set out to evoke.[1]

From this central view of art as contemplation one can look for qualities which are found only in works of art, and not in 'life'. The most obvious has necessarily been touched on: art adds to experience the sense of heightened and significant form. And here, at the risk of appearing reactionary, I should like to put in a good word for the author's intention in his work. A work of art is composed by a human author, and means to some degree the things he intended when conceiving and executing its form.

That this formula can be profoundly misleading there is no denying; some critics are so alive to its dangers that they talk of works of literature almost as though these were self-generated, or as though the artist had been superseded by his art. Northrop Frye, in his brilliantly searching *Anatomy of Criticism*, puts the argument strongly:

[1] There is one familiar aesthetic complexity which may seem to conflict with the views just expressed. This is, that some writers directly mime the contemplative experience, whereas others mime the spontaneous feelings and wrestlings of experience direct. There are poets like Marvell, Wordsworth and Philip Larkin, who recollect in tranquillity; their poetry enacts the meditating, and to this degree distancing, mind. And there are other poets like John Donne, Gerard Manley Hopkins and Ted Hughes, who wrestle dramatically with language and syntax, so that we seem to be at the white-hot point of experience itself. Dramatic art tends towards the illusion of immediacy and vitality; lyric art (perhaps also the epic) to the illusion of distance and control. But both have in common the fact that they *are* illusions. The basic difference between enacted and re-enacted remains the same.

The same is true of any other literary techniques which achieve the effect of immediacy – of the ironists who tease and disconcert us; even of Sterne, who seems to be breathing down our neck.

The absurd quantum formula of criticism, the assertion that the critic should confine himself to 'getting out' of a poem exactly what the poet may vaguely be assumed to have been aware of 'putting in', is one of the many slovenly illiteracies that the absence of systematic criticism has allowed to grow up. This quantum theory is the literary form of what may be called the fallacy of premature teleology. It corresponds, in the natural sciences, to the assertion that a phenomenon is as it is because Providence in its inscrutable wisdom made it so.

With the main tenor of this I have every sympathy, but the analogy Northrop Frye uses seems in one respect false. The author of a poem or a novel undoubtedly exists as a person, and not as an hypothesis; if one wants to know what he is like and what is to be known about him, it is for a biographer, not a theologian, that one will send. One can be certain that a work of art bears the stamp of human sensitivity and intelligence, and that some purpose was intended in it, of however enigmatic or controversial a kind. If this is admitted, the necessary reservations asked for by Northrop Frye can be conceded – that a writer's subconscious contributes to creation as well as his conscious, so that to this extent his 'intention' may be only the start. Perhaps he changes his intention in the act of creation, or perhaps the finished artefact is something he scarcely envisaged at all. The artefact has, after all, its own autonomy, and belongs to an order of literature as well as to an order of life. The words used in it, the myths and archetypes, belong to a continuing tradition; they have their own life, their own directions even, beyond the bending of a writer's will. The nearer a writer comes, moreover, to human experience, the more his myths and archetypes will take on the ambiguities and ambivalences of life. Is this particular character, we ask, like Lucifer or Prometheus? – is he hero, villain, scourge, scapegoat, or a mixture of all? The debate continues about Tamburlaine and Milton's Satan, about Becky Sharp and Ahab, as it would about their counterparts in life. All writers who touch upon the ultimate meaning of existence also move in this realm of flux. The disagreement about whether *King Lear* is or is not 'Christian' moves very close to disagreements about whether the Crucifixion is or is not a divine event. This, again, will remind us that emphases differ in recreating literature from reader to reader, and also from one generation to the next. Doubtless every new generation finds in the great works of art its own reflection; doubtless every individual reader contributes private insights and ideas and associations of his own. This area is certainly the one in which things get 'read into' literature – yet learning to distinguish between the inner resonances of a work and false interpretations is, after all, one of the things that criticism exists to achieve. When all these factors have been understood and allowed for, the author's 'intention' has not wholly vanished from sight.

So here is one positive difference between art and the raw material of experience: there is a guaranteed meaning in something made by a human being, in a human tradition, and with words. And this implies a second difference, no less decisive, but now (again) on the readers' and audiences' side: invariably we come to art with the general expectations of pleasure, interest and, even more importantly, beauty, which inhere in the very idea of meaningful form. We enjoy not only discerning, but entering into a pattern; and this is true not only when the work of art is about pleasing things and intrinsically delightful, but when the experience mediated is tragic or grim. The fuller implications of this paradox I shall return to; meanwhile, I want to call attention to a certain kind of superiority to people and events in literature which our expectation of beauty and interest necessarily confers. This is not in any sense moral superiority: it is, rather, the superiority of a god. We come to art with some degree of foreknowledge, and with a high degree of detachment from events. One obvious example of what I have in mind is 'dramatic irony'. We have some intimation of the immediate future when we know who is hidden behind the screen, or behind the disguise. Dramatic irony is only one aspect, however, of our varied special insights into people and events. There are all the numerous intimations of futurity mediated in a work's genre; in its myths and archetypes; in its ironic nuances; in its actual story, if this is public property; and, not least, in its implicit challenge to the readers to pit their wits against the writer, anticipating the aesthetic problems he has set himself to solve, engaging in whatever games he has implicitly chosen to play with *them*. For these and other reasons, it cannot be too often remembered that the pleasure of discerning moral values in literature, and even of acquiescing in them, is no guarantee of superior virtue in ourselves. A number of potentials are involved in it, some reputable and some disreputable, a few of which I should like to list. There is our intelligence in taking a point, for instance – perhaps morally neutral? Though for an intelligent man to use his intelligence is obviously more virtuous than letting it sleep. Then (to take comedy as an example) there may be pleasure in the downfall and humiliation of a sinner – morally vicious this? (unless we really are hating the sin and loving the man; or unless his sins are of an inhuman kind.) Allied to such pleasure, but now undoubtedly virtuous, is pleasure in the restoration and endorsement of social order, the vindication of those previously discriminated against or misunderstood. This may extend even to the redemption of the sinner, in which event the comedy may include intimations of a distinctively religious kind. And shot through all this is our delight in aesthetic pattern (morally neutral again? – though in that fascinating hinterland where the moral and the aesthetic meet).

But then again there are still more specific data. In comedy, to continue with this illustration, we have certain very precise expectations; that virtue (and youth) will be rewarded, despite trials and misunderstandings; that evil will be found out and confounded; that the wicked will be redeemed for the happy ending, or at least rendered powerless; that the natural movement is towards reconciliation, with festivities of marriage or feasting to crown the affair. All these expectations, if entertained in life, would be highly precarious; they might happen if we are lucky, but there is no possible guarantee that they will. The dogma that evil is always detected and virtue triumphant belongs either to wishful (or fearful) thinking, or to religious conviction, if one transposes it back from literature to life. From here then one sees the two broadly different ways in which comedy can be related back from literature to our normal affairs. Some will detect in it the fulfilment of our wishes and longings, and see it as an escape, or at least a holiday, from life. But others will recall that Hope is a Theological Virtue; and that the Divine Comedy contains and transcends the near tragedy of the Cross.

I have taken comedy as an example, since genre literature most clearly illustrates what I have in mind. But all great literature mediates some foreknowledge to its readers, as the six works used in this book have sufficiently shown.

V

For the final stage of this argument, I should like to focus attention on articulation, which is another basic aspect of literature, and possibly the most complex of all. Why do we need to articulate? Is it because we are egoists? Because we are sociable? Because silence would kill us, from frustration or boredom? Because this is what makes us king of the brutes? Is it because, having a useful faculty, we are bound to use it? Or because the human habit of talking is irresistibly strong? A complete theory of literature would need all the attempted answers and not just one of them, yet most answers are complex, and some mutually incompatible, especially when they are attempting to explain the psychology of articulation itself. There are areas of doubt about some of the most fundamental matters. As far as I know, the psychology of laughter is still a mystery. What emotions do we indulge, or refine, or catharsise when we laugh? A complete theory of comedy, satire and farce will have to wait for some fuller answers than Bergson gives.

The most basic answer to the question 'Why do we articulate?' is clearly, however, functional. Short of becoming Trappist monks or total recluses, we cannot escape communion with the world. And usually there is pleasure in even humdrum communication, of sharing opinions or having one's say. Even this 'pleasure' has its distinctive complexities; but it is only when we turn to premeditated and literary articulation that the problems familiar in literary criticism start to appear. To create literature is to generalise experience and dissolve loneliness; it is to offer something to the delight, and perhaps to the wisdom, of the race. For many writers it is also a compulsion, as sharp as any bodily desire. There is the urge to confront experience in language so as to sharpen it; to test and shape it, to explore, and, as Arnold said of culture, to make it prevail. And there is the urge to confer upon flesh-and-blood thoughts and emotions the more enduring incarnation of art. This may be primarily for the writer's own sake, or it may be for posterity's. Wordsworth's first concern, he tells us, was for his own older self, when the 'rememberable things' of youth might have grown dim:

I see by glimpses now; when age comes on,
May scarcely see at all, and I would give,

While yet we may, as far as words can give,
A substance and a life to what I feel:
I would enshrine the spirit of the past
For future restoration.

This kind of selfishness in the writer is, however, of universal interest; whether the later Wordsworth was helped by *The Prelude* or not, the Wordsworth who wrote it has put us all in his debt.

But what experiences lend themselves to 'enshrinement' in literature? Almost any we can think of; yet we might decide that they belong to two broadly different kinds. The first are moments won from, or distilled from, ordinary living, and to this degree the normal stuff of mimetic art. These can vary from powerful perceptions of love or death enshrined in exquisite lyrics to full-scale studies of human nature or society in 'realistic' novels by George Eliot or Zola, 'psychological' novels by James or Proust. The further literature moves in this direction, the more tempted we may be to forget its status as ordered and fictional creation and to imagine that the events and people are depicted directly from life. But the other kinds of experience which turn into art are more akin to mysticism, and to this degree not 'realistic' at all in any normal sense. They arise from moments of unheralded insight or vision, when a veil is lifted, and we feel ourselves to be greater than we know. These, perhaps, are moments which most compel towards articulation, through their challenge to stretch words evolved for everyday usage further than these will readily go. Those who have never mastered a distinctively creative medium may be familiar with the peculiar frustration of being unable to utter their most personal insights, and with the peculiar delight of discovering that others have uttered successfully on their behalf. It is profoundly reassuring, as well as clarifying, at certain exalted moments, to find that Wordsworth, or Virginia Woolf, or T. S. Eliot has been there before. Whether because we are compelled by some natural rhythm towards articulation and catharsis, or because as divine beings creation comes as naturally to us as breath, we need the songs of Sion in a strange land.[1]

---

[1] In distinguishing these two types of 'experience' for a pragmatic purpose, I am aware of the limited nature of their usefulness to aesthetic debate. I am by no means suggesting any absolute distinction between the 'realistic' and the 'mystical', but merely the difference between

So articulation has at least two aspects which are hard to separate; in crystallising emotion and thought it is a fulfilment, yet a fulfilment which is also a release and an escape. In this it is not unlike the sacramental consummation of sex in marriage, where fulfilled desire is also catharsis, but catharsis refines the cycle of desire and fulfilment in which it exists. Great poetry, Keats said in one of his axioms, has its natural rhythm:

> Its touches of beauty should never be half-way thereby making the reader breathless instead of content: the rise, the progress, the setting of imagery should like the sun come natural to him – shine over him and set soberly although in magnificence leaving him in the luxury of twilight.

And Oscar Wilde wrote this of tragic catharsis:

> Have you a grief that corrodes your heart? Steep yourself in the language of grief, learn its utterance from Prince Hamlet and Queen Constance, and you will find that mere expression is a mode of consolation, and that Form, which is the birth of passion, is also the death of pain.

We find in art, then, both the realisation of emotions and thoughts, and their catharsis; the artist himself is poised between the heightened experience he creates from, which may have its own exuberance, and the catharsis perfected, after the painful exuberance of creation, in what he creates. Henry James's Prefaces bear continuous witness to this vital duality; remembering the genesis of *The Portrait of a Lady*, for instance, he begins, as so often, from the charms of the city where he wrote:

> I had rooms on Riva Schiavoni, at the top of a house near the passage leading off to San Zaccaria; the waterside life, the wondrous lagoon spread before me, and the ceaseless human chatter of Venice came in at my windows, to which I seem to myself to have been constantly driven, in the fruitless fidget of

---

literature which concerns itself with closely observed and long-pondered phenomena, and literature which concerns things felt, seen, revealed or intuited 'in a flash'. The distinction relates, in brief, wholly to the world of experience which goes into literature, and not at all to the complexities (e.g. 'realism' versus 'fantasy') of literary form.

At the same time, all great works of literature incarnate uniquely and unrepeatably their creator's experience, and as artefacts are apt to become something like moments of revelation in their own right.

composition, as if to see whether, out in the blue channel, the ship of some right suggestion, of some better phrase, of the next happy twist of my subject, the next true touch for my canvas, mightn't come into sight.

Nothing here of Isabella's suffering and Madame Merle's deep treachery; only a haunting image of the enchanted city, and in James's creative ferment the restlessness, the unquenched expectancy of life. Northrop Frye's *Anatomy of Criticism* has a passage which is almost a gloss on this:

Most people, if they had just finished writing a play as good as *King Lear*, would be in a mood of exhilaration, and while we have no right to ascribe this mood to Shakespeare, it is surely the right way to describe our response to the play. . . . If any literary work is emotionally 'depressing', there is something wrong with either the writing or the reader's response. Art seems to produce a kind of buoyancy which, though often called pleasure, as it is for instance by Wordsworth, is something more inclusive than pleasure. 'Exuberance is Beauty' said Blake. This seems to me a practically definitive solution, not only of the minor question of what beauty is, but of the far more important problem of what the conceptions of catharsis and ecstasis really mean.

For the writer indeed there always is the gulf as it is defined by T. S. Eliot, between the man who suffers and the mind which creates. Yet this gulf, we must remember, is spanned by bridges; the man who suffers *is* the artist; he would suffer less as a man perhaps if he lacked the artist's honest and unqualified openness to life. And the art, when we have it, is an entirely new experience, of human suffering transmuted into the beauty and exuberance of form. Mr Alun Jones, in an article on the poetry of Robert Lowell, Anne Sexton and Sylvia Plath, has suggested a further possible variation on this theme. Just as the poet's suffering self, the *persona*, is like a seriously disturbed patient, so his creative self, the artist, is like the analyst, understanding and detached. The poem itself is therefore a kind of therapy – yet a therapy oddly qualified in that, though the poem may have a genuine wholeness, the writer's unhealed suffering seems to be required in some curious way for its aesthetic success. I mention this as an illustration of the possible complexities; but perhaps it is no more than an extension of the central aesthetic paradox of all literature, which offers beauty for ashes, turning transience and mortality to song, like the dying swan. We are most conscious of this transformation when the artists themselves draw attention to it – Tennyson and Baudelaire in poetry, Sibelius and Mahler in music – and it is interesting that they are apt to seem morbid when they do. Yet the transformation happens equally in artists who seem furthest removed from the morbid. What is more piercingly beautiful and hopeful than the St Matthew Passion? – especially when, as in its closing recitative and chorus, it moves us to tears. The transformation has, too, been the central insight of poems we do not feel to be morbid – Keat's Odes, for instance, or the Byzantine poems and the 'Lapis Lazuli' of Yeats.

VI

The writer's exuberance *is* the process of creating; this particular joy is denied to his readers, yet there is the answering joy for them of recreating and entering in. How often have we read something with a marvellously liberating sense of familiarity, as if we have always been waiting for it and only now are complete? Keats said of great poetry that 'it should strike the reader as a wording of his own highest thoughts, and appear almost as a remembrance'. Certainly poetry which does strike us in this manner has peculiar authority; we need less than usual persuasion to call it 'great'.

But such evocation, striking though it is, accounts for only part of the power of articulation in great poetry. There are many other pleasures, more accessible to critical formulation: the intellectual pleasure of understanding, the moral pleasure of judging, the spiritual pleasure of seeing individual experiences universalised in the union of beauty and form. It is in these activities that the recreation of literature produces an answering joy and exuberance in the reader; which is why reading should always, to my mind, be zestful and liberating, not crabbed and restrained. C. S. Lewis rightly insisted, in his delightful *An Experiment in Criticism*, on the need for surrender to literature and the others arts; only when we have entered fully into a work can we know whether it is going to be a possession for life:

We must not loose our own subjectivity upon the pictures and make them its vehicles. We must begin by laying aside as completely as we can all our own preconceptions, interests and associations. We must make room for Botticelli's Mars and Venus, or Camabue's Crucifixion, by emptying out our own. After the negative effort, the positive. We must use our eyes. We must look, and go on looking until we have certainly seen exactly what is there. We sit down before the picture in order to have something done to us, not that we may do things with it. The first demand any work of art makes on us is surrender. Look. Listen. Receive. Get yourself out of the way. (There is no good asking first whether the work before you deserves such a surrender, for until you have surrendered you cannot possibly find out).

What C. S. Lewis goes on to say seems to me supremely important. We value literature not only for what it says, or for what it points towards or teaches, but chiefly and most importantly for what it is. This is also the conclusion to which this book leads. If we are to value Shakespeare, it must in the first place be because he is Shakespeare; it must not be for anything we can paraphrase, or live our lives by, or in any other manner abstract. All these aspects have their place, and are indispensable; but creation itself, in art, is the supreme and rarest gift. The reason we value *Hamlet* is because it is *Hamlet*. Like Schubert's Ninth Symphony, or Ely Cathedral, or Michelangelo's David, it permanently enriches us. As long as we live, we shall return to it. It helps to make our life worth while.

So I would like to conclude with a final remark about art's transmuted experiences. The new creations of art are themselves experiences, and among the finest we shall ever know. In their marvellous energy they move human experience towards meaning and dignity, conferring their own special dignity of richness and form. There is a ritual, in all great art, of celebration, and not least in art which proclaims that the ceremony of innocence is drowned. And there is resonance in art, like the unforgettable resonances of experience: the sound of a piano across the piazza; the first lights in the Mall or the Champs Élysées; the fair, heard faint and raucous across the heath in summer; the eagles and trumpets. To remain blind and deaf to such things is to sink literature in 'realism'. It is to know nothing of the glory of art.

9 Between Two Worlds: Epilogue

> The soul of Man must quicken to creation.
> Out of the formless stone, when the artist unites himself with
> stone,
> Spring always new forms of life, from the soul of man that is
> joined to the soul of stone;
> Out of the meaningless practical shapes of all that is living or
> lifeless
> Joined with the artist's eye, new life, new form, new colour.
> Out of the sea of sound the life of music,
> Out of the slimy mud of words, out of the sleet and hail of
> verbal imprecisions,
> Approximate thoughts and feelings, words that have taken the
> place of thoughts and feelings,
> There spring the perfect order of speech, and the beauty of
> incantation.
>
> T. S. Eliot, Choruses from 'The Rock' (IX 16–24)

> And the Word was made flesh, and dwelt among us, (and we
> beheld his glory, the glory as of the only begotten of the Father,)
> full of grace and truth.
>
> John i. 14

In different situations and with different ironies, our six characters all endure agonies akin to Arnold's

> Wandering between two worlds, one dead,
> The other powerless to be born . . .

To this degree, I have suggested, they are paradigms of the artist in his depressed moments, wrestling to create order from chaos, torn between ideal possibilities and transience, tasting defeat. They could be taken as texts by those who see artists as creators of 'fictions' only – with all human attempts to make sense of life as unacknowledged fictions, and God himself as supreme fiction. Such theorists might claim some consolatory power for fictions, but can we really be consoled by lies? There might be some passing release of emotions, some temporary therapy, but no rest or repose away from the truth. If art is indeed the pursuit of impossible dreams, unattainable fulfilments, it mocks us as our six leading characters have been mocked. The world of the arte-fact merges with the scholar gipsy's Oxfordshire, with Aschen-bach's Tadzio, with Gatsby's Daisy: Mann's quotation at the head of my first chapter seems truer than Wilde's, fine though that is.

But even on this showing, there is a complexity; do our six characters really deserve fulfilment in their chosen terms? In varying ways they are weak or mistaken, mad, deluded or wicked; they are all trying to centre reality in themselves. They all seem to be lost in a labyrinth, though they see themselves as set on a quest.

Against these characters and their stories can be set the works which contain them; and here, we encounter much brighter truths. The artists do indeed achieve what they covet: aiming at beauty, they create beauty; aiming at order, they create artefacts wonderfully balanced and controlled. Since such works of art unite the soul of man with the world outside him, they are more substantial than mere fictions, or mere lies. They exist as symbols, apart from their makers; they belong, with nature itself, in the world outside.

The world of art is not spun out of a man as a spider's web is spun; it is not merely a report from the prison house. The soul of man is joined with the soul of form outside himself; and the transmutations of structure tug towards, not away from, truth. I agree with Coleridge in believing that successful works of art incarnate the human mind and spirit much as Nature incarnates the Mind and Spirit of God.

The essential aspect is that all revelation is enigmatic; there can be no simple union of the timeless with time. We live in a universe which bombards us with impressions, the most powerful and compelling of which are beauty, goodness and truth. These intimations reach us in a darkened form, in union with transience and suffering, and we move as strangers and pilgrims through their path. Always the spiritual qualities co-exist with mutability and enigma – not only in the world of nature, and of human creation, but in the supreme revelation of the Word. For a Christian, this is the quintessence of Incarnation, that God is really, if mysteriously, revealed in mortal flesh. The world of nature falls into place as lesser revelation; the world of art as the distinctive contribution of man.

Great art is not therefore 'between two worlds' in the manner of the six characters we have been following, but more as Christ was in his life on earth. When the soul of man quickens to creation it produces symbols: authentic and durable intimations of truth.

Index

'Abyss', the, 7–8, 20, 91, 94
Alice in Wonderland and *Through the Looking-Glass*, resemblance to Kafka's *The Trial*, 115–19, 125–7, 134
Ambassadors, The (James), 49
Anatomy of Criticism (Frye), 140–141, 147
Apology for Smectymnuus, An (Milton), 17, 98 n.
Arnold, Matthew, 4, 14, 41–52, 93, 114, 125, 144, 150: on Newman, 48; on Oxford, 47–9, 85; relationship with his central character, 6, 42; *Weltanschauung*, 44
Art as contemplation, 139–40
Artefacts, stress on, 12
Articulation, 144–8: catharsis, 145–146; exuberance and creation, 146–8; human suffering transmuted, 146–8
Aschenbach (*Death in Venice*), 1, 4–6, 10, 13, 81–99, 114, 138, 151
Augustine, St, 133
Austen, Jane, 137
Axel's Castle (Wilson), 88 n.

Bacchae, The (Euripides), 40, 87–90
Bacchic elements in modern life, 88–90
Bach, 11
Bacon, Sir Francis, 46
Baldwin, James, 89, 99
Baudelaire, 148
Beethoven, 11
Bellow, Saul, 100
Bergson, Henri, 144
Blake, William, 42, 147

Bleak House, 128
Brahms, 11
Brecht, 129
Brod, Max, 7, 8, 133
Bunyan, John, 116 n.
Burroughs, 8, 89, 99
Bürstner, Fräulein (*The Trial*), 121–122
Bush, Douglas, 18 n.

Cambridge Platonists, the, 20, 31
Camus, Albert, 89
Cargill, Oscar, 68
Carlyle, Thomas, 42
Carroll, Lewis, 115–19, 125–7, 134
Casebook on Henry James's 'The Turn of the Screw' (ed. Willen), 55 and n., 56, 60, 66–9, 71, 74–7, 79
Catharsis, 145–6
Changelessness of art, 9
Christianity and post-Christianity, 93–9: conditions of freedom mistaken for restrictions, 99; crude polarisation of alternatives, 94; fear of love, 97; overlooking of Christian aspect of love, 96–7; oversimplification of thinking, 94; rejection of the rejected, 97
Coleridge, Samuel Taylor, 151
Comedy, 136–7, 143
Comte, Auguste, 44
Comus (Milton), 2, 4–6, 9, 10, 13–40, 42, 95, 114, 132: Milton's relationship to Comus, 15; critical analysis, 15–16; Sabrina, 15, 16; the Lady, 5, 6, 10, 15–17, 19, 24, 27–30, 32–8, 95, 114; Nature

Comus (Milton) (contd)
and Grace, 15, 39–40; exaggerated importance of Epilogue, 15, 16; case between Comus and the Lady, 16–17, 19, 22, 26, 39–40; Chastity and virtue, 16–17, 24, 29–32, 38; Reason and Passion, 17–18, 22, 23, 25, 32; cosmos as harmony and chaos as disharmony, 18–19, 27, 28; use of rhetoric, 21, 22; grouping of characters, 24; the Attendant Spirit, 24–7, 32, 37; the Elder Brother, 24, 30–3, 37; virtue as knowledge, 25; results of loss of virtue, 26–7; Comus's pagan joy, 28; Comus and the Lady, 28–30, 34–8; Hell as a state of mind, 31; the Younger Brother, 32; central scene, 34–8; the first temptation, 34–6; the main temptation, 36–8; diabolical advocacy, 36; the Christian framework, 40; Bacchus's defeat by the Christian God, 40

Content and form, 2, 3, 8–10

Cox, C. B., 88 n.

Critic as Artist, The (Wilde), 1

Crucible, The (Miller), 74

Dante, 116

Death in Venice (Mann), 1, 7, 9, 11, 40, 81–99, 129; Bacchic aspect, 83–4, 86–90, 99; developments of imagery and theme, 84; image of Venice, 85–6; moral judgments, 90–3; the 'abyss', 91, 94; triumph of form, 91; intellectual framework of book, 93–9; post-Christian development of Aschenbach, 93–9

De la Mare, Walter, 135

Dell, Ethel M., 136

Dickens, Charles, 99, 136

Divine Comedy, The (Dante), 115

Donne, John, 98, 140 n.

Douglas (*The Turn of the Screw*), 59, 60, 72

Dover Beach (Arnold), 45

Dramatic irony, 142–3

Dryden, John, 22

Edwin Drood, 9

Eliot, George, 43, 145

Eliot, T. S., 9, 46 and n., 89, 93, 100, 101, 135, 145, 147, 150

Essays and Studies (Tillyard), 16 n.

Euripides, 40, 56, 87–90, 93

Evans, Oliver, 69, 71

Experiment in Criticism, An (Lewis), 148–9

Faerie Queen, The 38

Fagin, Nathan Bryllion, 67, 74

Finn, Huckleberry, 72

Firebaugh, Joseph J., 60–1

Fish, Stanley, 6

Fitzgerald, F. Scott, 4, 14, 100–13, 129: relationship with Gatsby, 6

Flora (*The Turn of the Screw*), 58, 60–5, 69

Form and content, 2, 3, 8–10

Formalist approach to art, 11–12

Forster, E. M., 13

Freud and Freudians, 94, 96, 97: Freudian interpretation of *The Turn of the Screw*, 67–9

Friendship as casualty of obsession with sex, 97–9

Frye, Northrop, 140–1, 147

Genet, 8, 89, 99

Gibbon, Edward, 73

God and the Bible (Arnold), 42, 43, 47

Goddard, Professor Harold C., 56–57, 79

Governess, The (*The Turn of the Screw*), 4, 5, 7, 13, 54, 58–79, 114, 130: critical defences of her, 66–68, 74; evidence for her insanity, 56–7, 61, 66–71; her knowledge, 60–4, 70; James's relationship to her, 7, 70

Gray's *Elegy*, 48, 50

Great Gatsby, The (Scott Fitzgerald), 4–6, 9, 13, 100–14, 129, 151: portrait of a broken society, 101–3; the rich and the working class, 101–3; the setting, 103–7; Carraway and Gatsby, 103–10, 112–13; illusion and reality, 111–112

Grose, Mrs (*The Turn of the Screw*), 55, 57–66, 72, 75–9

Guilt, refusal of, 130–3

Gulliver's Travels, 72

Hair, 99

Hamlet, 137, 146, 149

Heilman, Robert, 66–7, 69, 74

Hitler, 88

Hopkins, Gerard Manley, 140 n.

Hough, Graham, 12

Hughes, Ted, 140 n.

'Il Penseroso', 21, 48

Imagination: as alternative to personal life, 12–13; as divinity, 12–13

In Memoriam (Tennyson), 99

Incarnation, the, 151–2

Irony, dramatic, 142–3

James, Alice, 68

James, Henry, 3–5, 7, 9, 13, 14, 53–81, 129, 130, 145–7: on the House of Fiction, 53–4

Jessel, Miss (*The Turn of the Screw*), 57, 58, 60, 62–4, 66, 72, 73, 78, 79

Job, Book of, 115

John, St, 96, 150

Jones, Alexander E., 71–2

Jones, Alun, 147

Joseph K. (*The Trial*), 4, 5, 7, 10, 13, 115–25, 127–33, 138

Kafka, 2, 4, 9, 14, 114–34: instruction to destroy *The Trial*, 7, 133; search for religious truth, 127

Keats, John, 9, 146, 148; Odes, 48–49, 148

Kermode, Frank, 12, 88 n.

King Lear, 115, 133, 141

King's College Chapel, Cambridge, 11

Knight, Professor G. Wilson, on *The Scholar Gipsy*, 41–3, 48, 52

Lady Chatterley's Lover (Lawrence), 89

'L'Allegro', 21

Larkin, Philip, 140 n.

Laurel and Hardy, 136

Lawrence, D. H., 42, 89

Leavis, Dr F. R., on *The Scholar Gipsy*, 41–2, 45

Lerner, Laurence, 9

Lewis, C. S., 22, 148–9

Life and art, differences between, 136–7

Literature and Dogma (Arnold), 42, 47, 49

Little Dorrit, 128

Locke, John, 46

Lodge, David, 12

Love, 96–9: Christian aspect, 96–99; distinguished from sex, 98; modern fear of it, 96–7

Lowe-Porter, H. T., 81 n.

Lowell, Robert, 147

Lydenberg, John, 60

Mahler, 10, 148

Mailer, Norman, 99

Mann, Thomas, 4, 9, 12–14, 40, 81–99, 129, 151: indebtedness to Wagner, 84; on the 'abyss', 8, 20, 91; relationship with Aschenbach, 6

Marvell, Andrew, 140 n.

Marx, Leo, 100

Maxwell, J. C., 16, 29

Michelangelo, 149

Miles (*The Turn of the Screw*), 57–62, 64–6, 69, 75, 79

Miller, Arthur, 74, 138

Milton, John, 3–6, 9, 12, 15–40, 95, 98 n., 114, 120, 132, 141: and debate between good and evil, 19–24, 33; as moralist and artist,

Milton, John (contd)
6; personal relationship to Comus, 6; Platonic tenor of mind, 16–18, 26, 27, 38–40; Puritanism, 19, 25; theological view of human nature and history, 19; use of rhetoric, 21, 22; view of chastity, 16–17; 38–9; view of the Devil and his emissaries, 19–21, 36
Milton's Poetical Works (ed. Bush), 18 n.
Mimesis, 12, 136
Muir, Kenneth, 29
Muir, W. and E., 115 n.

Nabokov, Vladimir, 99
New Testament and acceptance of guilt, 131
Newman, Cardinal, 48
Newton, Sir Isaac, 46

Oedipus Rex (Sophocles), 133
Oh! Calcutta, 99
Old Testament, and acceptance of guilt, 130
Oliver Twist, 136
Othello, 136, 138
Oxford, Matthew Arnold and, 47–9, 85

Paradise Lost, 15, 19, 22, 23, 25, 26, 30, 31, 33, 36
Paradise Regained, 15, 22, 36
Pater, Walter, 49
Paul, St, 91, 93, 130, 133
Phaedrus (Plato), 82, 87
Pilgrim's Progress, The, 116 n.
Plath, Sylvia, 147
Plato, 82, 87, 93, 130
Platonism, 83, 114–15: Milton and, 16–18, 26, 27, 38–40
Polarities, 4: dramatised in human terms, 4; internal and specific, 3
Portrait of a Lady, The (James), 53–4, 146–7
Preface to 'Paradise Lost', (Lewis), 22
Prelude, The (Wordsworth), 145

Proust, 2, 145

Quint, Peter (*The Turn of the Screw*), 58, 60, 65, 66, 74–9

Rahv, Philip, 69
Rape of the Lock, The (Pope), 137
'Reality', 5–6, 136
Reed, Glenn A., 68
Rock, The (Eliot), 150
Rousseau, 131
Ruthven, K. K., 88 n.

Sacred Fount, The (James), 71
St Matthew Passion, 148
Salem children, the, 57, 74–5
Salinger, J. D., 100
Samson Agonistes (Milton), 15, 37
Scholar Gipsy, The (Arnold), 4–6, 10, 13, 41–52, 151: melancholy realism of the nineteenth century, 43–5; science and magic, 46; organisation of the poem, 48–52; myth of the gipsy, 48–50; symbolic function of the gipsy, 49, 51, 52; death as the reality, 51; a poem of unbelief, 52
Schubert, 149
Sense of an Ending, The (Kermode), 88 n.
Sex, modern obsession with, 89, 99: friendship as the chief casualty, 97–8
Sexton, Anne, 147
Shakespeare, 116, 133, 147, 149
Sibelius, 148
Silver, John, 77, 78
Smith, John, Cambridge Platonist, 31
Sophocles, 133
Spenser, Edmund, 38
Stanzas from the Grande Chartreuse (Arnold), 41, 45
Sterne, Laurence, 140 n.
Strauss, D. F., 52
Studien über Hysterie (Breuer and Freud), 68
Studies in Milton (Tillyard), 16 n.

Studies in the History of the Renaissance (Pater), 49
Surprised by Sin (Fish), 6 n.
Swift, Jonathan, 72
Symposium, The (Plato), 87

Tadzio (*Death in Venice*), 5, 81–3, 86, 87, 90, 95, 96, 98, 151
Talmud, the, 130
Tennyson, 52, 99, 148
Tillyard, Dr E. M. W., 17: on Comus, 16, 21, 27, 28, 38; on Milton's rhetorical powers, 21
Tolstoy, 136
Tonio Kröger (Mann), 13, 81, 82, 91, 95
Tragedy, art of, 137–9
Trial, The (Kafka), 4, 7–8, 114–34; resemblance to the Alice works, 116–19, 125–7, 134; Joseph K.'s arrest, 119–20; his first interrogation, 120; his insecurity, 120–1; the parable in the cathedral, 122–125; K.'s ordeals and emotions, 127–8; twentieth-century malaise as central theme, 128–34; K.'s character, 129–30; his refusal of guilt, 130–3; unfounded religions objections to *The Trial*, 133–4
Turn of the Screw, The (James), 53–80, 124: James's basic trick, 53–4; evidence for the Governess's insanity, 56–7, 61, 66–71; her knowledge, 60–4, 70; James's ambiguities, 66, 70, 91; critical defences of the Governess, 66–8; religious imagery, 66–7; Freudian interpretation, 67–9; virtuosity of the tale, 71; audacity of James's technique, 73; seriousness of the tale, 73; invocation of the Salem children, 74–5; two famous 'cruxes', 76–9

Ubu Roi, 88
Union of worlds in literature, 10–12

Van Doren, 68–9
Verdi, 11
Voltaire, 73

Wagner, 10, 84
Waldock, A. J. A., 76
Waste Land, The (Eliot), 101, 137
What Maisie Knew (James), 70
Wilde, Oscar, 1, 13, 146, 151
Willen, Gerald, 55 n.
Wilson, Edmund, 76, 88 n.
Wimsatt, W. K., 5
Woodhouse, A. S. P. on Comus, 15, 16, 39
Woolf, Virginia, 145
Word in the Desert (ed. Cox and Dyson), 88 n.
Wordsworth, William, 140 n., 144–145, 147

Yeats, W. B., 9, 13, 44, 85, 89, 148

Zola, Émile, 145